SAINTS IN TIMES OF TURMOIL

Saints in Times of Turmoil

by
JOHN V. SHERIDAN

Foreword

by

Cardinal Timothy Manning

PAULIST PRESS
New York/Ramsey, N.J./Toronto

CB
ShS

Library of Congress
Catalog Card Number: 76-39774

ISBN: 0-8091-2005-4

Cover Design: Nigel Rowlings

Published by Paulist Press
Editorial Office: 1865 Broadway, N.Y., N.Y. 10023
Business Office: 545 Island Road, Ramsey, N.J. 07446

Printed and bound in the
United States of America

Contents

Foreword by Cardinal Timothy Manning 1

Author's Note 3

Preface 5

1. Edel Quinn 12

2. Oliver Plunket 21

3. Jerome 30

4. Augustine 36

5. Catherine of Siena 43

6. Thomas More 49

7. Francis of Assisi 55

8. Thomas Aquinas 61

9. Elizabeth Seton 69

10. John Nepomucene Neumann 84

11. The Uganda Martyrs 98

12. Miguel Agustin Pro 112

Foreword

We in Los Angeles delight in the articulations of Monsignor Sheridan when he speaks and writes. There is a unique charm and depth to his words. We are especially pleased with this series of biographical vignettes on men and women who speak so eloquently to us, out of periods which parallel our own. We share them happily, knowing that they will bring souls closer to our heavenly Father, especially in "Times of Turmoil."

Timothy Cardinal Manning
Archbishop of Los Angeles

Author's Note

One night, after discussing the theological high-lights of Vatican II with a group of five or six hundred Catholics in a large parish in Orange County, California, I spent three weary hours answering questions that were almost repeats of ones I was receiving from my newspaper correspondents all over the country: "Has mortal sin gone down the drain?" "Were Adam and Eve myths?" "So masturbation is no longer a sin?" "My youngster was told in school that if she was getting nothing out of the Sunday Mass she had no obligation to go," "How much can the Church change and be the same Church?" "So we've succeeded in protestantizing our faith, giving up our heritage of Latin liturgy and chants for bad English and Sunday morning rock sessions," "Why are priests so disillusioned with their priesthood, nuns leaving their convents?" etc., etc.

Worn out by my patience-trying efforts to answer the same questions in a dozen different forms, and by the humiliation of discovering that my lecture fell so short of its objective, I apologized and told my audience that I would come back and help set up a regular series of adult classes on history, the Church, etc. The physician who introduced me remarked that it took a saint to stand up to all the questions "in times like these." "But maybe," he said as an afterthought, "living in times of change involves unusual sufferings, unusual opportunities for being saints. Maybe the question we should be asking is, 'Is it possible to be a saint today?' or 'How can I be a saint today?' Weren't there saints," he asked me, "who went through periods like

3

ours? Maybe next time we should talk about some of the saints who lived in *times of turmoil*."

I returned to that church to speak on St. Augustine. It was a much more satisfying spiritual adventure for all of us, including myself. Augustine had incarnated for my listeners a kind of God-relatedness, Christ-relatedness, Church-relatedness, people-relatedness, problem-relatedness, if you will, which suggested this volume of what is, hopefully, a today-oriented look at the saints.

Preface

Some time ago I glanced at an old book titled, "Saints Are Real People." I suppose the implication was that some of us feel the saints are not for real, or that they are presented to us in such a way as to make them seem unreal. We have formed some vague ideas of saints as superhumans, mythological figures, or worse, as masochists or milquetoasts. Too bad we do such violence to the word "saint," by which St. Paul meant a good honest-to-God Christian and which, etymologically, means a person of integrity, purity, sincerity.

Of course, we have used the term "saint" for the last several hundred years to refer to that great litany of individuals selected by the Church for the heroic, almost spectacular, way in which they lived their sainthood. But we should not apply the term "saint" only to those who have been canonized; they are a mere sampling of what all of us should be or try to be. True, the canonized saints include men, women and children of every temperament, every social grouping, every historical epoch and culture. The names they bear, their associations with people and times like ours, their personal lives, all have a significance for each of us. The Church canonizes them for their special witness, their singular sanctity, their intercessory powers, their ability to focus our attention on the communion of saints to which we are all called.

But what about the uncanonized saints, the ones we meet every day? The patient, hardworking mothers or fathers who have given their all to their children, often only to experience their children's indescribable sting of ingratitude? What about the dear old lady abandoned by her family, relatives and friends, alone and lonely in her squalid rest home bed, secretly hoping that God will take her from her miseries; the equally lonely and uncertain teenager wondering if she is really loved; nervous, anxious, unable to come to grips with her changing self? The once gentle switchboard operator bludgeoned into insensitivity by the cruel, callous, thoughtless phone callers who never pause to think that there's a human being like themselves at the other end of the line? The heartbroken father, mother or child watching hopelessly a loved one writhing in pain, about to enter the death agony? What about the suffering parents of the young woman kidnapped on the freeway, living with the agony and uncertainty as to whatever happened to her in the end; how did she die? What about the sick, depressed, impoverished men and women who, despite the grimness of their daily existence, force themselves to radiate a spirit of joy and gratitude, to live moment by moment, thinking only of others?

I suppose the author of "Saints Are Real People" was saying to his readers: "Are you one of those who have forgotten that saints are human beings? Have you just given up on saints? Ceased to believe in them, think about them, talk to them, pray to them? Are you forgetting that you yourself are a saint or a potential saint, that saints have all the problems, temptations, hangups of their fellow humans? Do you not realize that saints struggle with themselves just as you do? They struggle to do the right thing, to listen to the Spirit, to live at the summit of their spiritual, moral, social and intellectual powers. Do you forget that saints are phlegmatic, passionate, neurotic, that they number among them the physically handicapped, the psychologically and spiritually weak, that the only thing common to all of them is that they are saints, or want to be saints?

In this little book I've taken a brief glimpse at some of the best-known saints, seen what sort of people they really were, how human they were, seen the special problems they were called to face and how they faced them. The decade since Vatican II has been one of growing consciousness, growing insights into the life of the human spirit, growing awareness of the Holy Spirit's work in the Church and in each one of us. That same decade has brought enormous turmoil, innumerable crosses to a generation who had, perhaps naively, looked on the Church not so much as the Faith Community or Communion of Saints, but as the great problem-solver, the rock of certitude which stands firm and changeless against the storms and tremors of history, the solid anchor when everything around shudders and flounders. For such a disillusioned generation, as well as for a more modern one whom self-fulfillment eludes precisely because it has made self-fulfillment its life's goal, the saints, canonized and uncanonized, have an uncanny relevance.

The saints can seduce us to the only way of life which will bring us fulfillment. They can fill us with hope, make us grapple with ourselves, recognize ourselves for what we are, saints or potential saints called to the community of God through our own unique struggles, problems, pains, temptations. The saints make us aware that our very lethargy, our temptations, our sufferings, our joys, our frustrations, our enthusiasms are the stuff of sanctity. The saints bring home to us that we, too, are called to be saints through the kind of environment in which we are born, the milieu in which we grow, the people among whom we live. We are called to be saints through the very blood that flows in us, through our temperaments, through our hereditary weaknesses and talents. The things which identify us and make us different from all others are the things through which we become saints; that is just one of the lessons the saints have for us.

Some of my readers may not feel immediately at home in other cultures. They may find it difficult to capture the moods and tempers of other peoples, or other times. They may feel that our violent, technological age has no place for saints. Thus, I tried to select men and women whose essential humanness breaks vividly through their environments. I, myself, find it helpful to reflect occasionally on our common humanity, on the human spirit which I share with the Sumerians who have long since disappeared, and the Bostonians who, thank God, are still around. It was fashionable in the late sixties and early seventies to assume that the empirical thrust of contemporary thought, the temptation to quantify everything, makes God and the human spirit remote or elusive. There was the vague impression that all our traditional aspirations and values were in their death throes, that the essential mystery which we are called to live was somehow dissolving before the mind-blowing breakthroughs of contemporary science.

This kind of thinking narrows our historical perspectives, it forces us to see history only as a dynamic, not as a memory. It excludes the essential, the continuous in our human growth process. It makes us forget that our elementary reactions to the people and things around us so often echo those of a Jerome, or an Oliver Plunket or a Father Pro. I tried to put together a number of people with some elements of whose lives we can all easily identify.

In her "Saint Watching" Phyllis McGinley regretted that because of her poor education on the saints she did not encounter them as real persons when she was younger. She knew about Francis the Poor Man who called the swallows his sisters, she heard of Dominic who preached to the fish when no one came to hear his sermons in church. She asked Jude for impossible things and Anthony for help in locating her missing charm bracelets. It was only when she began reading history seriously that she came on the flesh and blood human beings whom we call saints. From then on, at every turn and twist of the years some saint emerged to enlarge her historical sense, to typify his own age and to incarnate the human ideals that instinctively occur and reoccur to all of us.

Phyllis complained that hagiography, or the art of writing about saints, was too often of the pious sounding and sanctimonious kind. But, she felt, that treated properly, with their faults and failings, as well as with their Christian love and exuberance, saints would always have a captive audience. I agree with Phyllis. The saints have said a lot to me over the years. I have found them very human, very much themselves, difficult to really imitate, but extraordinarily interesting as persons who had come to grips with their own instincts and with the environment in which they found themselves. I can still see that old Jerome striking out at his enemies, or those whom he felt to be the enemies of himself or his religion. I can hear his sardonic tongue, I feel enraptured by his biting language, glad that I was not around to be its victim. I can sense the old man's passionate disposition, cultured by a combination of God's grace, a strong will and sheer self-denial. I can feel the ominousness with which he watched the lights of the only civilization he had known and loved go out. I can listen spellbound to Augustine, that marvellously creative and convincing convert; I can gain immeasurable hope from him as I watch him breathe his last breath in joyful hope while the barbarians battered and ransacked his beloved Hippo. Everything he stood for seemed to be crumbling around him, but his faith-vision focused on the heavenly community to which we are all making our tortured way.

I can see Oliver Plunket, the seventeenth century Irish archbishop, and Father Pro, the twentieth century Mexican priest, returning to their persecuted countries, certain that they were exposing themselves to death, yet tireless and hope-filled to the end. Catherine of Siena taking the Pope to task for staying away from Rome. Thomas More accepting death with the warmth and humor of a great advocate resting his defense. Aquinas, the humble intellectual, protected by soldiers as he gave his inaugural lecture in the University of Paris. Elizabeth Seton, that dauntless woman, buffeted by one cross after another, yet rising above them all to build a great religious community, raise her own family and influence the lives of thousands of others. John Neumann, the humble German missionary grappling with all the problems of a new restless country, tirelessly ministering to the countless immigrants and confounding the nativist bigots. I can see Edel Quinn, the young, tubercular Irish girl travel all over East Africa to bring the people there the joy and love of Mary. I can see the young pages in a pagan court of Buganda rise above their environment like the early Christian converts, and go cheerfully to a dreadful death rather than repudiate a faith that had literally taken possession of them.

The saints listed here have a special appeal to me. They represent different milieux, temperaments, attitudes. The one thing they have in common is the exuberance of sainthood, something which is possible for all of us, something to which we all are called. I've put them together in the hope that you will find out more about them and that, finding out more about them, you will find yourself being a little more like them.

J.V.S.—1976

1. Edel Quinn
1907-1944

There are some people who, though not canonized, are recognized as saints by large groups of people who brush against them from time to time. They go through life, like our Blessed Lord, always doing good and, when they have passed away, their memories linger around like benedictions. Such a one was Edel Quinn, a contemporary of our own, a beautiful young woman whose life and spirit, so exquisitely sketched by Cardinal Suenens, can move its most hardened readers to rethink their own lives. Edel's biography should be better known. When he was Pro-Secretary of State for Pius XII, Pope Paul remarked that "Her (Edel's) kind of devotedness and supernatural spirit . . . should be brought to the knowledge . . . of all those who have at heart the advancement of devotion to Our Lady . . . of all those apostolic workers who in their various ways are working in the Father's harvest fields." "Unquestionably," he said, "this most attractive example (of saintliness) will draw numerous souls to the Church."

Edel Quinn was born near the little town of Kanturk, County Cork, Ireland, on September 14th, 1907. Because of her father's work as a bank employee, her family moved to several Irish towns, finally settling in Dublin. Edel received her elementary education in local convent schools. For her high school studies she went to England, returning to Dublin where she attended business school and received her diploma. An accomplished pianist, she also played tennis and golf and was a graceful dancer. Attractive, bright-eyed, alert-minded and personable, she was close to her family, extraordinarily selfless and intensely interested in other people, especially the poor and spiritually confused. She combined a sharp humor with business efficiency, genuine warmth and a sense of joy which didn't quite conceal an interior life nurtured by prayer and spiritual reading.

Her first job was with a French business firm whose young Dublin representative (a Frenchman) found himself, after some time, in love with Miss Quinn. As he later reviewed this one-sided love affair, he came to the conclusion that it was her sheer goodness and attractiveness that had unconsciously pulled him towards her. Though she apparently knew nothing about this, he took it for granted that once she recognized his love for her she, too, would become interested. But, unexpectedly, as he told her of his love, he saw "a pained feeling creep over her face"; then, in her own clear-eyed way, she told him she did not or could not share his sentiments. In fact, she had made up her mind to join the Poor Clares. The young man, now happily married and the father of a very successful family, shared with Bishop Suenens fifty letters which Edel had exchanged with him after this encounter. They glow with selfless love. Few young people could have kept this kind of correspondence without getting emotionally involved with each other. Edel's letters had a strange combination of warmth and discretion.

Through the ups-and-downs of a normal young life, Miss Quinn became manager of the Dublin branch of the French firm. She was, simultaneously, devoting herself to her family, her friends and those whom she felt were in need of her help. She put on plays for deprived youngsters. She visited hospitals and orphanages and, finally, through an interesting series of coincidences, she came into contact with the Legion of Mary, then in its infancy, and became an active member of a Praesedium whose chief work was rehabilitating prostitutes. While she threw herself almost totally into the work of the Legion, she kept up many of her social contacts, her family closeness and her regular work schedule. Edel also attended daily Mass (she had an extraordinary interest in the Liturgy) and did quite a lot of spiritual reading. Her tireless work, coupled with her complete self-forgetfulness, may have contributed to her generally frail physical condition. At any rate, a medical checkup revealed that she was in the advanced stages of tuberculosis and she was compelled by her doctors to spend eighteen months in a sanitarium. Her reactions to hospital confinement were noticeably undisturbed. She never lost her serenity or humor though she knew her tubercular condition would prevent her entering the Poor Clares.

As she completed her hospitalization the Legion of Mary was attracting worldwide attention and its Dublin headquarters were being called on to send its representatives all over. Edel, though still an invalid, volunteered to do extension work in England. Initially turned down, she persisted. All she wanted, she said, was a chance to make Mary and her Legion known to people whose lives were spiritually empty. This could be her vocation. Now that she could not become a member of the Poor Clares she could penetrate the dark, congested areas of English streets where people were looking for the kind of inspiration and encouragement that the Legion could give. She went to England for a few weeks and her success there convinced both herself and the Legion people that this was her work. As she returned from England a request came from the Legion envoy in

South Africa for someone to introduce it in the eastern and central parts of that continent. She wanted to go.

In September of 1936 a Dublin newspaper carried a brief story on an Edel Quinn; she was, it said, to be the Legion's new envoy to East and Central Africa. It did not say that it was over the objections of a large number of legionnaires that the Dublin headquarters voted for her to go to Africa for a period of three years. But, with the vote, was a unanimous expression of concern about her health. Basically unperturbed by her frail health, Edel was delighted to be chosen for Africa. She made a second pilgrimage to Lourdes, returned to Ireland and began her long voyage, via England, to Mombasa, East Africa. Met in Mombasa by the Bishop of Zanzibar, Miss Quinn was sent on to Nairobi, a more central location from which she could begin the work that culminated in her final union with Christ and Mary. Her extraordinary powers of observation, her eye for scenic detail, her love for and openness to all people, regardless of race, color, belief or unbelief, shine through her large collection of shipboard and African letters.

It was in Kiambu, a well-known Kikuyu mission center (on the outskirts of Nairobi) that I first read the copies of her letters quoted in Suenens' biography. I was so affected by them that I read the entire biography one night by the light of an African moon. Initially I couldn't help but wonder how a young Irish woman would feel in such a strange environment. But, unexpectedly, her description of her first Christmas in Kenya radiated a joy, love and enthusiasm that could come only from God. She was an affectionate girl with a special love for her family; she was able to channel it into an equally strong attachment to her African sisters and brothers.

God had given her extraordinary resources. "Notwithstanding the goodwill of a very small group of friends," wrote the veteran missionary Father Reidy, "Edel faced a gigantic undertaking practically alone. But her outward manner never showed this. Her cheerful and happy disposition carried a light-heartedness which was infectious. She was ever alert for the humor of life. She laughed and made others laugh; but behind all was her single-minded commitment to making Christ and Mary known to the people to whom she was sent." Father Reidy remarked that the idea of a woman missionary was a surprise to Europeans and "To the Africans it would normally seem absurd." "But," he added, "their prejudices melted like snow under a tropical sun the moment they met with her. Her selflessness and her love caught them so much off-guard that they felt totally at home with her and identified immediately with her cause." "Besides," he said, "the complicated character of her work, far from alarming her, seemed to take on a simplicity as she moved serenely, working fourteen and fifteen hours a day, to bring her message in Swahili, Luganda, Kikyuyu, Luo, Luhang, Kimaru and Kikiamba."

The priests who came into contact with Miss Quinn testify that their lives were somehow transformed by hers. Always humble, loving, humorous, she nevertheless exuded a goodness and truthfulness that could only be explained by her interior union with Christ and His Blessed Mother. She had words of praise for everyone around her, yet she was very frank about their responsibilities. "The Legion of Mary," she said to one priest, "is what its Spiritual Director makes it. This is particularly true in Africa where the people look to the priest to know what Christ and Christianity mean in their lives and his."

A briefest glance at the enormous distances which Edel Quinn covered by ship, train and, mostly, in a broken-down car, staggers one. Times beyond number her "Rolls-Royce," as she called her battered jalopy, was caught in the mud of roads that disintegrated under the tropical rains and she had to make her way on foot through the lonely, impassable tracks to the nearest mission. On other occasions she would write her letters in the old car as she waited for help to get it out of the mud. The present Kenya, Uganda, Tanzania, Zambia, Malawi, South Africa—they were part of her massive beat. Her letters take them as much for granted as a group of neighboring Irish villages. She returned to convents and mission houses at one and two o'clock in the morning, often sleeping on their verandas in the mission compounds, rather than disturb the nuns. Aware of her physical weakness, and knowing that she did not have long to live, she was determined to keep going until the end. She did not want any reports of her ill health to go abroad. Indeed, two things she was most opposed to: personal publicity and comments on her health.

Cardinal Suenens describes Edel's movements against a background of constant crises. World War II was reaching agonizing proportions in Europe. The Nazi machine was rolling relentlessly over Belgium, Holland, France. Africa, too, or parts of it, were in turmoil and its European missionaries were being cut off from correspondence with their families. Dublin grew anxious about Edel. It was assumed there that her movements in Africa would be restricted because of the war; so it was suggested that she might go to the Philippines or even to China. Her response: "Whatever happens and whatever be the consequences, don't worry about me." It was getting difficult, she admitted, to get through Africa with the lack of gasoline and the perils of ships at sea, but she was determined to cover all the vicariates before leaving it.

Though she seemed to love life, death had no fears for Edel. Her concerns were her African legionnaires and her own family whom she did not want to sadden. "A very grave Spiritual Director asked me," she wrote Dublin, " 'Do you realize you are dying? Have you made your preparation?' He asked me so many questions," she said, "I finally had to take him seriously. That's why I am compelled to tell you that I am ill. Though I feel I should not be bothering you." When she had heard that she was reported dead and had all sorts of Masses said for her, her response was: "The trouble is that when I do really go people will have tired praying for me."

Fearing that the Legion of Mary would suffer by her illness, she asked Dublin to think of someone for her place in case she couldn't continue. Her request, coupled with a report that she had entered a sanitarium in Johannesburg, upset them at home. But, true to her concern that her sickness wouldn't bother anybody, she blotted out the word "sanitarium" from her hospital stationery; her letters were all concerned with the success of the Legion.

After a few months' hospitalization in Johannesburg she headed back to Nairobi, back to her original mission. Though she was "completely worn out" (September 1943), weighing less than eighty pounds, she undertook a six-weeks' Legion tour, retracing her earliest footsteps. On February 29th, 1944 she developed a chill and was taken to one of the convents; on March 6th of that year she took to bed for the last time. She had reached such a state of exhaustion that everyone around her felt that her death was imminent; this despite the fact that she had had some extraordinary recoveries in the past. But she continued to see visitors, write reports, encourage her legionnaires. On May 8th and 10th she had a couple of death-like attacks and rallied to the point of planning to move to another convent for a week's rest.

On May 12th, the day she arranged to move, one of the sisters brought her a new dressing gown for which she beamed her gratitude; she was given some light refreshments, which she described as "delicious," and only moments afterwards she called the Mother Superior to say she was weakening and ask, "Mother! Is Jesus coming?" Jesus came soon: that evening as the sisters and fathers recited her beloved "Hail! Holy Queen." She was buried in the missionary cemetery in Nairobi. Her funeral was enormous; they came, blacks, browns and whites, from all over, to bid her a fervent farewell. Why shouldn't they? She was one in whom they had never failed to recognize a real sister in Christ. Word of her death spread from Africa to Rome to Dublin, and to the whole missionary world.

One of Edel Quinn's first letters aboard the Llangibbi Castle that took her on her great missionary journey was addressed to Frank Duff, the founder of the Legion of Mary. It is reproduced in the Suenens biography. "I couldn't say thanks," she wrote, "when I was leaving as I was afraid of breaking down, but let me say it now. It is good to feel one is trusted. It will be a help in the days to come. *I would like you to remember always whatever happens* that I am glad you gave me the opportunity of going. I realize it is a privilege and also that only you persisted I would never have been sent. I only hope I do not fail the Legion when the work comes to be done. I am counting on all the prayers to counteract that danger. Whatever be the

consequences, rejoice that you have the courage to em-
ulate our Lord in His choice of weak things, in faith.
Any sorrow caused to others was worth it. Remember,
I knew that you felt pretty badly that others were suffering; but have no regrets. I am not going to refer to
this again. I am glad you let me go—the others will be
glad later.''

Edel Quinn was just twenty-nine years of age when
she wrote this letter. She was leaving a family who
loved her intensely, a host of close personal friends and
a full life. Rome is now in the process of reviewing the
heroic record of that life. We may not anticipate what
Rome's final decision will be, but two things we can
say: the woman who wrote those prophetic words had
something of the saint about her, and those of us who
come in contact with her cannot but be better for it.

2. Oliver Plunket
1629-1681
(Feast Day: July 11)

To the Irishman, and to a lesser extent to the Britisher, the name Oliver is highly evocative. The Britisher will take pains to prove that the arch-fanatic Oliver Cromwell was as cruel to his fellow Englishmen as he was to the Irish. Of course the Irish do not believe this. They can find nothing in history, or at least in their reading of it, to compare with Cromwell's Drogheda massacres.

There is another Oliver, to whose Drogheda shrine the Irish have flocked for many years. They sought his intercession daily; they prayed for his canonization and they filled the piazza of St. Peter's on October 12th, 1975 when he was finally and officially declared a saint of the Universal Church. He is St. Oliver Plunket, scion of the great Anglo-Irish family of that name, seventeenth century Archbishop of Armagh, Primate of Ireland, and last of the Tyburn martyrs.

I was in Drogheda for the 1974 pilgrimage which included a rosary procession, a concelebrated Mass and a blessing with the reliquary which enshrines the martyred archbishop's head. I had a special interest in Oliver Plunket. Just forty years before, in a hospital not far from Drogheda, I lay dying of tubercular peritonitis; the doctors had sent my father and a priest-friend of the family to inform me of the fatal character of my illness and to tell me that I should be dead within a few days. Despite my great pain and discomfort, I was initially shocked by the news, but soon disposed myself for the death I thought inevitable; indeed, I wanted to get it over with as quickly as possible. An old nun (who died on the Monday before his canonization) began a novena of prayer to Oliver Plunket for my recovery and, through eighteen months in the hospital and three years with a punctured intestine, to the supreme bafflement of my doctors, I recovered.

Oliver Plunket's Ireland had all the ingredients for the making of martyrs. Poverty- and violence-ridden, completely without hope, its people were hunted like wild animals. Its Gaelic civilization was brutally sapped out as if it were a poisonous thing. Its lands were expropriated. Its last soldier-defender, Owen Roe O'Neill, had fallen. Its earl-chiefs, fusion of Norman and Gaelic blood, had fled to the continent. The Catholic Confederation was a dismal failure, the Catholic King James was routed at the Boyne and Ireland's last resisters to its tyranny were bleeding to death from the never-to-be-forgotten scourge of Cromwell. Oliver Cromwell had completed his Drogheda carnage only two decades before Oliver Plunket returned from Rome.

Plunket, born in 1629 near Oldcastle, County Meath, was educated by his kinsman, Patrick Plunket, the Benedictine Abbot of St. Mary's, who later, as Bishop of Meath, ebbed out his life in a Dublin hiding place. Oliver and three fellow students went to Rome with Father Scarampi, Innocent X's envoy to the Catholic Confederation. He completed a distinguished course at the Irish College, Rome, was ordained in 1654 and remained with the Fathers of Charity, working among the poor and incurables; he also took degrees in canon and civil law, became Roman representative of the Irish bishops and one of the city's great professors.

In 1669 Oliver was selected by Clement IX to replace the Irish primate who died in exile in France. To avoid antagonizing the anti-Catholic authorities in Ireland, he was consecrated in Belgium and, a few months later, began his heroic Irish pastorate. Prayer, service, sacrifice, hard work, ecclesiastical organization; endless visitations to the sick, sorrowing, broken people while he himself was hungry, cold and physically exhausted; such was his life. The Ireland in which he labored was like an accursed wasteland whose people had nothing but their faith; even their faith was being bled by factions and dissensions that would make today's polarization among Catholics mere kindergarten play. In Plunket's twelve-diocese Province there was only the old Bishop of Meath left—in hiding. Derry, the scene of so much contemporary violence, hadn't had a bishop for a whole century.

Within Oliver's first six weeks' ministry as Archbishop he confirmed ten thousand men, women and children. In five years he had confirmed fifty thousand. In ten years he had spoken to and comforted hundreds of thousands of his scattered people, introduced fresh forms of discipline among a clergy who were harrassed, often uneducated, and vulgarized as freaks and castaways. He brought the Jesuits to Drogheda where he established a college, kept up an endless series of correspondences with Rome and called several synods, two within three months of his arrival in Ireland. He did these things, as a contemporary put it, "without any fixed churches or oratories and while celebrating the Mass and sacraments in open fields, in woods and in caves with the wind and rain for their setting."

Oliver's family background was such that were it not for his Catholic faith and priestly vocation he would have been one of his country's leading citizens. There were indeed times when, despite the ruthless persecution of Ireland's Church and its ministers, his family's influence was enough to make the politicians wink at his missionary work for his dejected co-religionists. But there were times, too, when he was compelled to travel in a variety of disguises that in retrospect give a cloak-and-dagger excitement to his movements. Now a country squire, dressed to match such a one, now a high-ranking British officer, with wig and sword, riding over the fields and ditches of his native haunts; now a cattle merchant, passing casually through the rank and file of his persecutors to carry out his priestly work in the bogs and hedges, recognized only by those who sought his spiritual ministrations.

A vivid letter writer, Oliver's own description of his missionary life in Ireland reads like a page from an ancient martyrology: "The hut in which Doctor Brennan (Bishop of Waterford) and myself have taken refuge is made of straw," he wrote. "When we lie down to rest we can see the stars through the openings of the roof and when it rains we are refreshed even at the head of the bed by each successive shower." Describing another situation, he wrote, "We arrived at the house of a reduced gentleman who had nothing to lose. But, to our misfortune, he had a stranger in the house, by whom we did not wish to be recognized. Hence, we were placed in a large garret without chimney and without fire, where we have been during the past eight days; may our sufferings redound to the glory of God, the salvation of our souls and of those of the people entrusted to our charge." And, "So dreadful has been the hail and cold that the running of the eyes of both my companion and myself has not ceased yet. I feel I shall lose more than one tooth so frightful is the pain they give me. My companion is attacked with rheumatism in one arm so he can scarcely move it."

It would take some knowledge of Irish and English history to understand the inexorable rush and complexity of the forces that were closing in on Oliver Plunket from the day he returned to Ireland as a Catholic archbishop—indeed, from the day he was born. The Norman conquest of England was completed in 1016. Just 150 years later (1170) England's Henry II, with the alleged permission of the English Pope, Adrian IV, began the invasion of Ireland. For better or worse, that invasion was never really successful. Its obstacles included a wholly different kind of civilization, a complicated clan system with a highly detailed legal arrangement for the protection of human rights, for land tenure and for local government; an ancient language, and the Catholic faith, which was to survive the Reformation, Henry VIII's nationalization of the Church and the Cromwellian rebellion.

The early Anglo-Norman conquerors fused with the local Irish chiefs, making it necessary for England to contrive all kinds of legal and physical schemes to keep its foothold in Ireland. Legislation was enacted forbidding the English "degrading" themselves by getting involved with the "mere Irish," their customs, language, dress, liturgy or law. By the time of Henry VIII the English part of Ireland had dwindled to a small section around Dublin. But with Henry and his greedy cohorts began in earnest the literal destruction of the Irish as a people; it involved wiping out their language and religion, vesting their property in the Crown, replacing them with English and, subsequently, Scotch adventurers.

England operated in Ireland both directly and through a vice-regal amalgam of loyalists and place seekers in Dublin Castle. All this meant that among other things the intricacies of English local politics, including its nationalization of the Church, its Cromwellian revolution and its Jacobite or Stewart wars, became an integral part of Ireland's problems. Oliver Plunket's attempt to be a real pastor to his oppressed people made him a scapegoat for the endless variety of fears and hostilities about alleged plots and counterplots (Titus Oates, the Popish Plot, the Gunpowder Plot, etc.) that, rampant in England, spilled over to Ireland. In Oliver's day a Catholic could be hanged in London for being a Catholic, while in Ireland the original Tories (Gaelic, "pursuers"), the dispossessed Irish, were massacring every new English land holder they could get their hands on. Archbishop Plunket was caught in this demonic net. As a Catholic bishop he was always subject to arrest and punishment; and though he condemned the Tories, both he and his fellow bishops were constantly accused of siding with them. His seizure and imprisonment while visiting the dying Bishop Plunket in Dublin was something which could have happened to him at any time. The miracle was that he was able to have ten such extraordinarily fruitful years. Heroic priests like himself kept the faith alive in Ireland through centuries of the bitterest oppression. Only men of his stamp could dramatize for a plundered and impoverished people the supreme value of their religious faith. St. Paul asked, "What can a man give or get in exchange for his faith?" The Irish could have retained their freedom and their lands if they had given up their faith. It was that simple.

After his arrest in 1679 Oliver was taken to Dublin Castle and held incommunicado for seven months while a coterie of perjured witnesses, including a couple of dissolute friars whom he had disciplined, were gathering to swear that he had plotted to bring the French into Ireland. The charges were so ludicrous that even the prejudiced Dublin jury had to drop them, but through the conspiracy of a Cromwellian bishop and Lord Shaftsbury his case was transferred to England where he would have no defense. He was taken in chains to a cell in Newgate Jail in London which had just been occupied by the martyred Provincial of the English Jesuits.

Plunket, like Thomas More, was a skillful lawyer; he demanded that he be allowed to bring his witnesses from Ireland. But, because of insufficient time and contrary winds, they never got there. His judges and crown lawyers who protected their lying witnesses from cross-examination openly browbeat him in court. "I have come here," he protested, "where no jury knows me or the quality of my adversaries . . . Your Lordship sees clearly that I do not have the time to bring my records or my witnesses." And the Lord Chief Justice confessed: *"The heart of your treason was the setting up of your false religion,* than which there is nothing more displeasing to God or more pernicious to mankind, a religion that is ten times worse than all the heathenish superstitions." Never was anyone a more explicit victim of religious persecution.

The barbarous penalty for treason was that the culprit be strangled and, while still alive, cut open, his heart torn out and thrown into the nearby waiting fire. Oliver foresaw the painful horrors of this monstrous kind of torture. "I expect daily," he wrote to his nephew in Rome, "to be brought to the place of execution, where my bowels are to be torn out and burned before my face and my head is to be cut off. But," he said, "it is a death which I embrace willingly. Compared to the death of the Cross it is but a flea bite." (He had more than a touch of Thomas More's humor.) On July 1st, 1681 he was tied to a horse's tail in Newgate and dragged through London to die at Tyburn, the only bishop to die there and the last of its martyrs. "And being the first (primate) among the Irish, I will teach the others," he wrote, "by the Grace of God and by my example not to fear death."

On his way to the scaffold Oliver paid special tribute to the love and compassion of his English friends who had come to help and comfort him. It was typical of his own love, his gratitude, his generosity. His suffering at the hands of some English politicians was no stigma on the noble Englishmen who stayed with him to the last. They were the saints, the fellow humans, the brothers, the ones who following in Christ's footsteps came to visit him in his hour of trial, while some of his own were swearing his life away. But Oliver prayed for those too. Paul VI on the occasion of his canonization described him as, "The advocate of justice and the friend of the oppressed; he would not compromise with truth or condone violence. His constant plea was for pardon and peace. He would not substitute another gospel for the Gospel of love and peace. His words of love and pardon rang from the scaffold on which he was about to hang, they were words of blessing and forgiveness: "I forgive all who had a hand directly or indirectly in my innocent blood.' O what an example, especially for the Irish people of whom he was one and to whom he ministered."

Even while Plunket's canonization was taking place another chapter of his country's tragic history was being written in blood. The people of Northern Ireland were locked in bitter and barbarous conflict whose religious overtones served only to scandalize a world that needed desperately the example and inspiration of people like St. Oliver. "Let the canonization of Oliver Plunket," said the Pope, "be a proclamation of peace and reconciliation to his people; let his work for truth and justice, his last appeal for love of neighbor, be emblazoned in the minds and hearts of his beloved Irish people."

On the morning of Oliver's canonization rain fell in torrents over the Vatican. As the ceremony began the clouds dispersed and the sun shone until the majestic liturgy came to an end, the voices raised in prayer were stilled, the sounds of music died away and the two hundred thousand pilgrims filed down through the piazza, out under the Bernini columns and back to the hotels and hostels of the Eternal City. There was prayer and hope in their hearts that the clouds of frustration, despair, violence and hate that darkened the Northern Ireland skies would give way to the love, peace and reconciliation which was the life and lesson of St. Oliver Plunket.

3. Jerome

c. 343-420

(Feast Day: September 30)

For native querulousness, sheer invective, deadly wit and sarcasm, St. Jerome has few peers; certainly none among the canonized saints. Though committing himself, after his famous vision in the desert, to abandon the classical authors with whose language he was so infatuated, he wielded Latin with Ciceronian dexterity. Indeed, it is doubtful if Cicero himself had Jerome's capacity, either as a wordsmith or polemicist. For, like O'Casey, Shaw, Frank O'Connor and the innumerable other Irishmen whose brilliantly nuanced English make native English writers wince, Jerome's Latin wed the classical with the colloquial, giving him a uniquely lucid and devastating instrument of expression.

The English scholar, Ann Freemantle, translated and compiled Jerome's "Satirical Letters"; though a tiny sample of his loaded missives, they are gems of diatribe. Despite his terrifying irrascibility, his passionate temperament and his pitiless satire, Jerome was a harshly disciplined scholar and an authentic saint. He was as merciless with himself; indeed, he was much more merciless in his self-imposed forms of mortification than he was with those against whom he flung his most fiery verbal darts. A gourmet taste with a sensitive stomach, and a fairly indulgent period of adolescence, were a singularly poor preparation for the parched rocks of the desert where he made his home and scrambled for the tasteless morsels of food which were to be his chosen diet for several years.

Jerome's great objectives were to live the poverty and privation of Christ, to tame his naturally unbridled spirit, to develop a Christian monasticism and to make the scriptures come alive in the idiom of his time. Despite his endless embroilment with pagan and heretic, with friend and enemy, he succeeded in transmitting to posterity God's word in all its flaming brilliance and an image of himself as a supremely complex and passionate man who made a total commitment to Christ.

Dalmation by birth, Jerome was schooled in his home town, near the modern Ljubljana, Yugoslavia, and went to Rome at the age of twelve where he lived what he, probably exaggeratedly, described later as a dissipated youth. Though neither he nor his contemporaries were interested in recording the personality traits or vagaries of youth, one thing is certain about his student days in Rome: he worked extremely hard in the cultivation of the Latin classics, rhetoric and the other scholarly pursuits of the period and carried through life the memory of great teachers whom he idolized and immortalized. A Christian who loved the Roman basilicas, Jerome, following the custom of his time, was baptized in adult life, probably by Pope Liberius, about 366 A.D.

After his baptism Jerome left Rome for Treves, on the French Moselle, where the new Emperor Valentinian had set up his camp and court in the hope of stopping the Vandals at the Rhine and protecting his great city and empire from its eventual ruin. From Treves, where Jerome became interested in monasticism, he returned to his Dalmatian homeland, formed

a sort of religious community there and, after a dispute
with his confreres, left for Antioch where he suffered
an almost fatal illness. The illness was a crisis point at
which he made the somewhat rash promise never to in-
dulge in the classics again. Between 325 and 327 he
lived in the Chalcis desert near Antioch. He learned
Hebrew from a Jewish convert, had copies made of as
many Christian manuscripts as he could get his hands
on and carried on an interminable correspondence. He
involved himself in a bitter struggle between the episcopal contenders for the See of Antioch, kept in contact
with Pope Damasus and was ordained to the priesthood
in 378 on condition that he could keep his monastic
vows and would not be forced into pastoral work.

From Antioch Jerome went to Constantinople
where he studied Greek under Gregory Nazianus,
boned up on his Hebrew and returned to Rome to become secretary to Pope Damasus. On Damasus' initia-
tive he wrote exegetical tracts, translated several sermons of Origen and the Latin Fathers, revised the old
Latin version of the Gospels on the basis of the best
Greek manuscripts, and made his first revision of the
Latin Psalter. During this, his second round in Rome,
he conducted scriptural classes for a well-known circle
of matrons, taught them Hebrew, answered their biblical problems and became their spiritual director. But,
due to his attacks on clergy, lax monks and dissipated
virgins, and to some calumniators who unjustifiably
suspected his relationship with his women instructees,
he left Rome in a huff and made his way to the Holy
Land, accompanied by a group of his spiritual proteges.
He examined the archeological sites of Palestine and
Egypt, spent a month with the famed exegete Didymus
and settled in Bethlehem where, under his direction, a
monastery and guest house for men and women were

erected. Jerome lived in Bethlehem until his death in 420.

Aside from his enormous spate of letters, commentaries, sermons, controversies, biographies and personal conferences, Jerome's most immortal work was his translation of the Old Testament from Hebrew into Latin, and his revision of the old Latin version of the New Testament. His Latin Bible, known as the Vulgate, was until recently the Church's official version.

There is something almost embarrassingly contemporary about the personal, spiritual, psychological and social problems which Jerome describes and comes to grips with. To students of history, of language, of Latin, of polemics; indeed, to all those who want to feel the intense human problems that were experienced by so many people during the death throes of the Roman Empire and during one of the most elemental transitions in the Church, Jerome's writings will ever be a source of exhilarating interest. One can still hear him lashing out at Rufinus, his erstwhile friend, "You are the stammerer of the Latins. You teeter like a tortoise. You don't get any place. Write in Greek, for heavens' sake. Those who don't know the language won't know the difference."

His address to the lecherous deacon, Sabian, and his many paramours, including a nun, is a classic of censure: "I refuse to mention here the staggering number of virgins you are said to have seduced, the ladies of the aristocracy who violating their marriage by taking you as lover were publicly executed by the gladiators for your adultery. The filthy houses of prostitution, the hells you have crowed in like a rooster. . . . But contemptible Sabian . . . even these enormous sins are trivial compared with your seduction of the nun (within the precincts of the shrine of Bethlehem). First

you promise to marry your unhappy victim . . . you
snipped a few locks of her hair, and took a few hand-
kerchiefs and a girdle as a pledge of her dowry, swearing you would never adore another woman as you
adore her. Then you hastened to the place where the
shepherds had watched their flocks and the angels sung
overhead—there once again you pledged your troth. I
say no more. I do not accuse you of kissing or embrac-
ing her. No outrage is beyond you, but the sacred nature of that stable and that field forbids me to think
you are guilty except in your will and your heart."

Jerome's memorial against Bishop John of Jerusa-
lem is another example of his pungency: "You are the
most disdainful of bishops. You despise laymen, dea-
cons and priests and boast that you can ordain a thousand clergy in an hour. Your sycophants claim that you
are more eloquent than Demosthenes, more spiritual
than Chrysostom, wiser than Plato and, being a fool,
you believe them." When he took after Origen he told
him, "No need for wrinkling your nose, pulling your
hair or tapping your feet. . . . you are odious enough
without such tantrums." But Jerome recognized
greatness, even in those with whom he found it necessary to quarrel: "These are difficult times," he told
Augustine. "I have preferred to hold my tongue rather
than to talk. I have had to interrupt my work and, in
the words of Appius, to employ the eloquence of dogs.
But, as for you, I want to pay eternal tribute to your
genius. I am resolved to love you, to honor you, to support you and to defend your words as if they were my
own."

Though considered a misogynist, Jerome surrounded himself with women. He admired them when
they committed themselves to Christ and persevered in
their vocations, and he held those up as examples of

virtue. "Farewell, Paula!" he cried as he concluded his eulogy on that well-known sister. "Help your aged friend with your prayers. United now with Christ through your faith and your works you can obtain what you ask. I have built you a monument more lasting than bronze. I have engraved your epitaph for your tomb. I have put it here as a postscript so that wherever these, my words written in your praise, may go, their reader shall know that you repose in Bethlehem."

Jerome had no doubt about the transient character of flattery. He told the truth himself and wanted to have the truth told to him. A man of the utmost integrity, he was able to say before he died, "Only when our clay has returned to the clay that formed it and death has swept away authors and their critics alike, when the autumn leaves have fallen and a new foliage has appeared, only then will we be judged on our merits and not on our ranks. Posterity does not care a hang whether the author it is reading was a bishop or a layman, an emperor or a lord, a soldier or a slave, clad in silk and purple or covered with rags. It is not on titles. It is on merits that it judges a work."

Posterity has reserved a very special place for Jerome. The Church has called him its Doctor (teacher). The greatest of the Latin Fathers, he is witness to man's capacity to rise above himself and his times; he is a challenge and a comfort to those of us with bad stomachs, choleric tempers, troublesome imaginations and a lot of temptation.

4. Augustine
354 - 430
(Feast Day: August 28)

During a recent trip to Rome a priest companion
and myself started out for the ancient port city of
Ostia, but were side-tracked at the da Vinci airport by
a couple of limousine-stranded friends whom we had to
drive back to Rome. We were bound for Ostia because
of our love for Augustine and his mother, Monica. It
was on an autumn day in the year 387 that Monica died
in Ostia as she and her recently converted son were
about to embark for their native Tagaste, now Souk
Ahra in Algeria. To read St. Augustine's description of
his mother's death, and of the vision of heaven which he
shared with her nine days previously, is still an unforgettable spiritual experience. I remember like yesterday
my first contact with it: An old, scholarly teacher,
wanting us to know something of the beauty and sub-
tlety of Augustine's Latin prose, introduced us to his
Confessions. My own mother had just referred to Monica's deathbed request to be remembered by her son at
the altar when, by a happy coincidence, the teacher
asked me to translate from the Latin, Augustine's plea:
"Inspire O Lord my God, inspire your servants, my
brethren and my masters whom with voice and heart
and pen I serve, that so many as shall read these Confessions may at Your altar remember Monica."

For fifteen hundred years no literate Christian has

gone through life unaware of or uninfluenced by Augustine. And it is my personal conviction that no Catholic student today should live his own faith crisis without knowing something of Augustine's intense process of self-discovery, his massive spiritual resources developed through a tirelessly inquiring mind, his feeling for man at man's most elemental level and his ever-growing union with Christ. Besides, the radically changing age in which Augustine lived, as well as his extraordinary genius, his great humanness and his high degree of holiness give him a singular significance for us young or older products of a changing milieu. He fused in himself a personalism, an existentialism, a realism that is as up-to-date as yesterday's encounter and as old as Adam's struggle to rediscover himself and his God.

The Africa in which Augustine grew up, a rich, commercially well-developed and sophisticated Roman colony, was seething with such a racial, ethnic, social, economic and political ferment that it would make our age seem like one of supreme tranquility. Rome's conquest of that northern belt of Africa was characteristically thorough, but its armies, secret police and wealthy colonists lived in constant fear of riots by the Phoenicians, Berbers, Ethiopians and the whole immense mass of displaced peoples who were boiling with discontent and a spirit of rebelliousness characteristic of so much of today's world. Add to this the fact that at the very zenith of Augustine's manhood the Visigoths were tearing down proud and imperial Rome itself, the African Church was rent in two with schism, and drunkenness, bribery and corruption of a thousand different kinds were rampant all over that province. One of Augustine's letters comments on how a group of Donatist Christians spent Ascension Day drinking; even some of their nuns, he said, were drunkards.

Augustine's whole life, his whole voyage of self-discovery, of discovering God and of bringing his fellow humans to God and Christ takes place against this dark and confusing background of changing systems, changing values, changing life patterns, changing attitudes. He literally watches one civilization in its death throes and another barely beginning to rise.

Augustine's youth was spent with his parents in Tegaste, his early adolescence in the scholastic town of Madauras and his young manhood in the University of Carthage where he joined the Manichaeans and, typical of his time, took unto himself a mistress who later gave birth to one son. His mother, a devout Christian, had succeeded in keeping him in some kind of contact with the name of Christ; his father was a pagan. Following the normal custom, Augustine was not baptized as a child. After a relatively successful start in the broad fields of law and rhetoric, he suffered a growing disillusionment with the basically unspiritual and anti-intellectual character of Manichaeanism and drifted into agnosticism. Through a book of Cicero (Hortersius, now lost) a series of contacts with students of neo-Platonism and a few devout convert friends, he began to take a serious look at Christianity.

In sheer frustration, to satisfy his intellectual and spiritual thirst and in search of a more fulfilling kind of work, Augustine went to Rome and from there to Milan where he was attracted to its great Christian teacher and bishop, Ambrose. His initial interest in Ambrose was the bishop's eloquence. Ambrose, aware of this infatuation, admonished his student that the supreme objective of all eloquence, all human search, must be God and Christ.

Augustine, always searching, always friendly, gathered around him a group of young intellectuals; they were seekers like himself; many of them had become Christians; each found Christ through his own singular circumstance; each responded to God's call in his own special way. All this time Monica was praying for her son. One day while he was sitting in his garden in Milan with his friend Alypius, Augustine felt himself torn in two by the need to make a final spiritual commitment. Suddenly he heard what sounded like the voices of children chanting (as in a game), "Tolle et Lege, Tolle et Lege" (take and read, take and read). Instinctively he turned to a copy of St. Paul's Epistles which he always kept on his table, and which was now in his garden. "Not in revelling and drunkenness, not in debauchery and licentiousness, not in quarrellings and jealousies, but put on the Lord Jesus Christ and make no provision for gratifying the flesh and its desires." These words, like a flood of light, illumined his path. His decision was made to enter the Church. He completed his teaching contract, went with his mother, some pupils and friends to the house of a colleague and after a few months of prayer, meditation, discussion and writing he returned to Milan where he, his son Adeodotus and his friend Alypius were baptized on the vigil of Easter, April 24, 387.

Augustine's mother's death delayed his return to Africa, but finally back at his native Tagaste he sold his family properties and organized a monastic community in which he hoped to spend the rest of his life. But God wanted him to live otherwise. On a visit to Hippo, the present Bona, about fifty miles from his home town, Augustine was seized by a group of people who had heard the bishop there appeal for an episcopal assistant. Reluctantly, he accepted ordination to the priesthood and three years later, on the death of Hippo's Bishop Valerius, he took over the See of Hippo; an incredible change took place in his whole life pattern now. Though he lived as much a community life as he possibly could, he gave himself totally to the pastoral office for which he had felt himself so unprepared psychologically and intellectually. Through forty years he preached, he wrote, he labored, developing a theology of the faith, living, searching out and prayerfully articulating the mystery of Christ in His Church, the "Whole Christ."

Augustine's own faith and theology were transfused and illuminated by the faith of the simple, generous, humble, dissipated, weak and responsive people of Hippo. He entered heartily into their devotional life. The literary fruits of his pastoral labors are so massive that they form a gigantic library as well as a heritage of faith and theology that makes himself, his life and works dominate early Christianity, linking it with our own most up-to-date theologies. Possidius, his earliest biographer, asks if any one man could ever read all of his books. One hundred and thirteen books, two hundred and eighteen letters and more than five hundred sermons still survive. Yet, over the period when Augustine was writing or dictating this immense theological library he was living the life of a religious, travelling over all North Africa to deliver his famous sermons, to participate in dialogues and debates and to present the Catholic viewpoint in some of the most famous councils in the early Church. His kind of pastoral work was much more varied and complex than that of today's bishop. He had to act as a judge for his people, both in civil and ecclesiastical affairs. He had to counsel them both personally and as a community.

Due to a simplistic and uninformed approach to his Confessions, Augustine comes across to some people as a mere youthful philanderer who spent the balance of his life repenting of his sexual offenses and giving his readers a too harsh view of those kinds of sins. Actually, Augustine's sexual offenses were little different from those of his contemporaries. His differences from them lay in his high I.Q., his profound sensitivity and his intense self-consciousness which expressed itself in his restless search for his life's meaning, or for what we would call today his "identity."

Augustine's Confessions are not a series of prurient self-revelations; they are a litany of prayerful thanks to Almighty God for God's self-revelation to him. No one knew better or said better than Augustine that in discovering God, a man young or old discovers himself. "God," he said in so many ways, "is more intimate to me than I am to myself." It was providential, however, that Augustine should choose for one of his works the confessional form. That form is what makes him so well known. In no other literary form could we meet on such intimate terms this warm, passionate, brilliant, weak, self-deceptive, proud, penitent, humble and grateful fellow human. Through no other medium could we follow so intimately this incarnate evolution of Christian thought, this spiritual crucible in which the religion of the New Testament blends with western Platonic tradition, giving it the spirit and depth of God's word, canonizing it; many of the fundamental thought patterns we use in Christian theology today can be traced directly to the grace-filled mind and heart of Augustine.

Augustine is often accused of excessive concern with sexual sins, of a too harsh theory of predestination and of endorsing or giving in to the physical persecution of religious dissenters. It is unfair to brand him this way; it is the sure mark of those who have no historical sense. The age in which Augustine lived, his personal background, his native sensitivity and the circumstances in which he spoke, demand our most sympathetic reflection; without this we cannot know him. To know Augustine is to love him, to admire him, to follow him, to follow him to the very end when, weakened with work and worry, he closed his long and prayerful life. As he died the Vandals were battering down the walls of his See city. In those last hours a lesser man could see or feel nothing around him but darkness. But Augustine's faith, his love, his sensitivity to God's presence, filled him with joy and hope to the end.

5. Catherine of Siena
1347 - 1380
(Feast Day: April 30)

It was recently suggested by one of the more moderate women's libbers that Catherine of Siena be chosen as the movement's patron. Though Catherine has left to us an extraordinarily rich reservoir of spiritual writings—at least 400 letters and a full-size book—in none of them do we find any discussion of the social or psychocultural status of women; but, of course, this does not nullify her claim to a special place among those who would elevate women to the summit of their human potential. Anyway, the subject of women's status would not have come up in 14th century Siena where it was simply taken for granted that a single girl should never go outside her home alone after the age of twelve and where women in general were treated as vassals, to be used, directed and controlled by their families.

Catherine, a twin, the twenty-third child of Jacopo Benincasa, a dyer, and his wife, Lapa Piagenti, was born in 1347 A.D. in relatively poor circumstances. Her mother, a normal product of the social patterns of the period, took it for granted that her daughter, a gay, spritely child, would either marry or join an enclosed Religious Community. But Catherine had a religious experience at a very early age which marked the beginning of her life as mystic and activist, a life far beyond the ken of her parents and contemporaries.

As she and her brother Stephen were returning home from a visit to one of her married sisters, she suddenly saw in the sky, over the towering St. Dominic's Church, what looked like an outline of the Glorified Christ with Peter, Paul and John. Catherine from then on cultivated long periods of silence, fasting and prayer and she informed her family that she had made a promise to Christ to follow Him in a special way. Her mother, a practical kind of woman, could not understand; she was upset with Catherine's departure from normal childhood behavior and insisted that she prepare herself, as the other girls in the neighborhood, for marriage or the convent. But, encouraged somewhat by her father, Catherine continued her own strange kind of vocation. She also let her mother know that her promise (though certainly not binding on a child of her age) involved a life of celibacy; and she even went to the extent of having her hair cut to symbolize her determination not to get married.

For the next three or four years Catherine lived a prayerful, quiet, introverted kind of life, working feverishly as a maid in her own home, leaving it only to go to Mass and devotions in St. Dominic's. Connected with the Dominicans in Siena was a large Third Order whose members were all older people; they met regularly, worked for the church, visited prisoners and helped the poor. Catherine decided to join that community of tertiaries; initially they turned her down because of her youth. But, helped by a Dominican priest who checked her background and intentions, she finally succeeded in joining them. Almost immediately her apostolate far outstripped anything the tertiaries had ever dreamed of. She prayed, she visited the sick, the prisons, the poor. She gathered around her an enormous number of followers who listened with rapt attention to her highly developed spiritual insights. Her followers included men, women, priests, politicians and representatives from all the social groups in Siena.

Catherine's family home, located in the Fontebranda, the working class district of the city, was attracting such a heterogeneous group of people that she became known (jokingly to some) as the Queen of Fontebranda, the "mother" of the great "family" of followers which was to form the Siena school of mystics. She was their authentic spiritual director. Under her influence they rebuilt their personal lives and formed a group of spiritual and social workers whose interests and influence extended far beyond Siena. Catherine's own confessor, spiritual director and, later, her biographer, was Father Raymond of Capua. With his fellow Dominicans he helped her theologically, but she had a depth to her spiritual life that could come only from her own vivid consciousness of God's presence, her own closeness to Christ, her own disciplined and living response to the Spirit. "Be sure, Father," she wrote to Father Raymond, "that naught I know concerning the ways of salvation was taught me by mere men. It was my Lord and Master who revealed (Himself) to me. . . ."

In a life of personal privation Catherine enjoyed a visible radiance and peace that held those to whom she spoke and ministered. She was determined to bring that peace to others. Her formula: "To love God (in ourselves and others) without moderation."

Among the social evils attacked by Catherine and her followers were the very serious family embroilments which were a mark of that period. While those domestic cleavages did not culminate in divorce, they had a traumatizing and embittering effect on all the families of the area. Interfamily quarrels were commonplace, as were the bloody wars between the local cities and states. Catherine threw herself into the work of bringing peace to the disturbed families of her own area. She gave spiritual direction to her co-workers and, never able to write well, she dictated her mystical theology. Because of her extraordinary impact on both the grandees and the poor of Siena, her influence inevitably extended to the wars between the states. Thus she was drawn into the debacle between Florence with its Italian allies and the papacy. This was fought out while the Pope was living in Avignon, the French residence of the papacy for seventy years. Catherine had from the beginning two objectives in mind; one was to bring the war between the papacy and the Florentines to an end; the other was to bring back the Pope from Avignon to Rome. The papacy's years in Avignon, often referred to as the Babylonian Captivity, was a period of great trial for the Church, especially for its leadership. In Avignon it was impossible for the Church to pursue unhampered its spiritual responsibilities without becoming enmeshed in the most bitter and selfish kind of international intrigue. Even nationalism was beginning to make itself felt at that time. Kings, emperors, princes and local magnates struggled desperately to use the Church, and many of the popes were either too weak or too willful to fight back. Catherine was convinced that the Pope should be back in Rome, and, the popes themselves wanted to get back, though every attempt they made to do so was foiled by one political incident or another.

Through her correspondence with him, Pope Gregory XI got to know something of Catherine's great spirituality and her extraordinary socio-political influence. She visited him at the behest of the Florentines and, while she did not succeed in ending the war between them and the papacy, she concentrated on getting the popes back to Rome, a city which was then falling to ruin. The French cardinals who had determined that the Pope should remain in France did their best to get rid of Catherine; they even succeeded in delegating a group of bishops to question her orthodoxy; those men spent a full day interrogating her; she emerged unshaken. Finally, on September 13th, 1376 Gregory left Avignon for Rome by boat; Catherine left the same day for Siena, taking the overland route. It was an almost miraculous victory for Catherine; the most dramatic of her achievements; yet one whose immediate results were to give her little solace. The Church which she loved was merely in the midst of its calvary. Avignon was bad; worse was to follow.

Gregory's health broke down. He was succeeded by Urban VI, a reformer who, tragically, antagonized everyone around him. The cardinals who had elected him decided (too late) that his election was invalid; they claimed to have been pressured. And thus began the forty years which we know in history as the Great Western Schism; it rocked the Church to the very verge of collapse. More than most, Catherine could see its horrors. She went to Rome to elicit support for Urban VI, but due to the humanly unhealable conditions of the papacy, the breakdown in her health and the terrible despair of her followers as a result of what was happening, she, after a period of illness and exhaustion, met her death on April 29th, 1380. Her body bore the stigmata. She was to know the redemptive power of prayerful suffering.

In a Church that has canonized men and women of every class, temperament, interest and vocation, Catherine is exceptional. Her complete departure from the ways of young womanhood, her unconventional life style, her sheer influence over such a great variety of people who, in the context of the time, would never defer to one of her age, sex or social status; her frankness, fearlessness, persistence and courage; above all, her profound spiritual insights and her determination to live and communicate them in the most depressing conditions—these are just some of the unusual facets of a 14th century woman who is indeed as contemporary as women's lib, war, and Watergate.

6. Thomas More

1478 - 1535

(Feast Day: July 9th)

The son of a judge and with a background that he described as "Not famous, but honest," Thomas More was born almost five hundred years ago in Milk Street, London. "The brightest star," said Thomas Fuller, "that ever shined in the via Lactea." Educated in St. Anthony's school in Threadneedle Street and in the home of Archbishop Morton of Canterbury, More was sent to Canterbury College, afterward Christ Church, Oxford, and transferred at the behest of his parents to Lincoln's Inn where he began the study of law. From 1500 to 1504 he lived with the Carthusians and once contemplated remaining in that community. Indeed, throughout his life he preserved many of its austere habits, including wearing a hair shirt, sleeping only five hours a night, partaking sparingly of his diet and spending a lot of time in prayer and meditation. His self-discipline and cheerful acceptance of suffering were rooted in his early and highly developed spirituality. "Featherbeds," he said, "are not the way to heaven. Our Lord Himself went hither with great pain and many tribulations."

While the law remained More's profession, his philosophic, literary and humanistic bent and achievements brought him into an international circle of scholars, including Erasmus, who lived with him while visiting in London, and bitterly complained that "England's only genius must of necessity devote so much of his time to the legal profession."

As a young member of Parliament, "a beardless boy," More resisted Henry VII's financial excesses, incurring the king's anger. Marrying Jane Colt in 1505, he then raised four children before she died in 1511, when he was espoused to the widow Alice Middleton, seven years his senior. A writer, lecturer, linguist, lawyer, diplomat and great humanist, More was irresistibly drawn into the public life of London where he became its Undersheriff in 1510 and represented its merchants abroad on several occasions. In the famous May Day riots, when a London mob attacked the foreign merchants, he restrained the rioters but afterwards formed part of the delegation which sued the king's pardon for them. It was typical of his humanity. More lectured on Augustine, composed Latin verse and during his 1515 ambassadorship to Flanders wrote Book II of his famous Utopia, describing a communist city-state whose institutions are governed by reason; he contrasts it with the godless policies of Christian Europe rooted in the gross selfishness and greed which he outlines in his Book I of Utopia.

Thomas More's sense of justice and objectivity, his deep spiritual insights, his Christlike sensitivity to the hypocrisy of his fellow politicians and his historical perceptiveness of the dangerous transition through which England and Europe were passing make him indeed a man for our season. Those of us who are Catholics quite naturally think of him in terms of his devotion to the ancient Church, his strong, silent disapproval of his king's divorce, his concern for the fragmenting influences of the Reformation and his uncompromising opposition to Henry VIII's cutting England away from its spiritual unity with the rest of Europe. But More's fear of Henry's arbitrariness was rooted at a far deeper level of history, politics and human freedom. More saw clearly that once Henry resisted successfully the papal challenge to his (Henry's) total autonomy, England would be submerged in an actual tyranny.

More's milieu bore many resemblances to ours. The Renaissance had created psycho-social and intellectual disturbances as deep as those of today's technological developments. The breaking up of Christendom must have been a frightening specter for thoughtful statesmen. The discovery of the New World has been compared with that of our journeys to the moon. More was very conscious of what those happenings could mean to human society if they were to be manipulated in favor of political adventurers. He was terrified by Henry's breaking with the political restraints that had developed during the Middle Ages; restraints, incidentally, that many of our contemporary historians fail to appreciate. Up to Henry's time it was assumed that even the king was subject to God and the law, that he was subject to custom, to the rights of the nobles, clergy and commons. The peasants had their well-established social and economic niches, their rights to common lands, for example; and the monasteries, despite their abuses, were conscious of and committed to certain forms of voluntary poverty and almsgiving. The theory of the two swords, that of the Church and the State, placed definitive limits on the king's scope of authority and prevented him from interfering in an area of human freedom which the Church was committed to uphold.

More saw that Henry was determined to wreck this traditional division of powers and thus control the

whole range of his subjects' human behavior. More was
too sophisticated, too much of a humanist, too much of
a European, too honest and insightful not to recognize
the blatant greed and Machiavellian character of
Henry's mentality, as well as the danger of vesting in
him, or any monarch, such totalitarian power. He could
not afford to support the king's shuffling off the Pope's
rights. It's not that he had more implicit trust in individual ecclesiastics than in laymen; he had resisted
Henry's involvement in the papal wars and cautioned
him against some of the Pope's secular policies; he had
denounced abuses in the Church's administration, but
he recognized in the man who was putting himself
above law and morality a dictator under whom the
freedom of the common man was forfeit.

More reached the highest position of any man,
apart from the king. Honors came rapidly and rested
lightly on him. He was knighted and made Under-
treasurer; he was Speaker of the House of Commons,
Steward of Oxford and Cambridge, a Justice of the
Peace, a reader of books whose anti-Catholic contents
could constitute a threat to the unity of the country.
During all his public years More ran a truly Christian
household. He indoctrinated his family in charity and
almsgiving. Prayers were said at his table and chapters
read from Holy Scripture and the Fathers of the
Church. No idleness was allowed, no gaming, no dic-
ing. Everyone was encouraged to pursue useful occupa-
tions and learning. He was one of the first fathers to in-
sist that the girls in the family be exposed to the entire
range of education which the sons received.

Henry VIII sought out More's company. More
had everything to gain from catering to him. The king
tried to force his first minister to declare his marriage
void, to acknowledge him as "the singular protector

and supreme lord." More was such an exacting and perceptive statesman as well as a Christian that when he was called to appear at Lambeth in 1534 to confirm by oath the Act of Succession which declared the king's marriage with Catherine void, and that with Ann valid, he was perfectly willing to acknowledge that Ann was now the de facto annointed queen. But he refused the oath as then administered because it entailed a repudiation of papal supremacy and prepared the way for a dictatorship.

It is inspiring to reflect on More's sensitive appreciation of what was happening in his country, on how seriously he took his official and personal responsibilities, and with what apparent ease he could yield up his life in defense of his principles. During his imprisonment he wrote a "Dialogue of Comfort," a devotional and humorous defense of those persecuted for following their conscience; in it he affirmed with great conviction that the head of a state cannot dictate religious belief. He also wrote a treatise on the sufferings of Christ; but before he could finish this work his writing materials were taken away from him; his letters of farewell and encouragement to his family and friends were scrawled with charcoal. More's public life was that of a great statesman; his words in the Tower were those of a mystic. He was both.

In 1534 the Act of Supremacy established the king as supreme head of the Church of England without reservation, and the Treasons Act made it high treason to deprive the king of his title. For refusing the oath, Acts of Attainder were passed against More and John Fisher, Bishop of Rochester. More's lands were seized and given to the crown. The Carthusians who refused the oath were condemned to death. Fisher was beheaded on June 22nd, 1535. More was interrogated in April, May and June of that year and, in Westminster Hall, he was charged with refusing to affirm the king's supremacy, corresponding with Fisher during their imprisonment and denying that Parliament could make the king the head of the Church. More, the perfect lawyer, defended himself on the plea that he had not spoken against the supremacy and that no law makes silence punishable. If, he said, silence implies consent, as the old legal axiom assumes, then his silence had approved rather than denied the statute. But he insisted that the Church throughout Christendom is one and indivisible; it is not within the power of one realm to make laws for it without the consent of the other. To do so, he said, would destroy the unity of the Christian faith and rob men of their freedom.

More was beheaded on Tower Hill on July 6th, 1535. But mindful to the last of Christ's example, he put aside the cup of wine offered to him on his way to the scaffold saying, "My Master had easell and gall, not wine, given to drink." His final words that he "die the king's good servant, but God's first," sum up his life and political career. His head, like those of all condemned "traitors," was placed on London Bridge. A mere handful of public men like Thomas More could renew the world. That such a man could rise to the political eminence he attained is itself a source of enduring hope. He was canonized May 19th, 1935.

Thomas More, a man for this our season.

7. Francis of Assisi
1181 or 82 - 1226
(Feast Day: October 4)

While in Rome in 1951 an Episcopal priest from California told me he was travelling with a group which included a young man who had just lost his wife. The widower was so distraught that the earlier part of the trip had no effect on him. In fact, it seemed to worsen his loneliness and anguish. Disappointed, the pastor took him away from the group for a full day's visit to Assisi. "We had scarcely completed St. Francis' Prayer for Peace in the Franciscan convent crypt," the priest told me, "when my friend seemed to experience a new feeling of joy. He was somehow identifying with Francis. As we made our way back through the hills he confided to me that he had lost complete contact with Christ since his high school days. 'I feel,' he said, 'Francis is now showing me the way back.' " I met that priest once again in a Los Angeles hospital. I reminded him of the incident and he told me that the young man had returned to the Church, was married happily again and was one of St. Francis' greatest apostles. The priest took a copy of St. Francis' Prayer for Peace from his wallet and handed it to me. "Our friend," he said, "prints thousands and thousands of these and gives them out to everyone with whom he comes in contact."

It used to be said that St. Francis experienced

heaven during his life on earth and that he was the only saint whom every generation and every religion since his time agreed to canonize. A bitter agnostic friend of mine, whose love for Pope John gave him the inspiration to visit Rome and Assisi, told me that the only prayer he ever said with sincerity was the Prayer of St. Francis.

Many years ago I began an article on St. Francis by saying that it was almost impossible to rescue the real Francis from the endless legends through which he comes down to us. I would never say this again; it takes the legends, the myths, the atmosphere of the troubadors, the scenic beauty of his Umbrian hills, the quiet of Assisi—it takes all of them to bring forward the real Francis as, under God, they all helped to develop the real Francis. It was by living and giving, poverty, chastity and obedience, the romantic flavor of the troubadors and the courts of love, that Francis captured the imagination of his time.

But Francis was no mere romantic; he was a Christian realist. Thus Christian realism, genuine love and simplicity became the new foundations for the ardor and romance of that complex age. While religious and social cranks of all kinds make him their Patron, while he has won the hearts of the sentimental, while traditional lovers of nature and contemporary ecologists have chosen him as their model, while peaceniks have turned to him with increasing ardor, St. Francis' authentic devotees, like the young Episcopal widower, will always find in him the way to Christ, the love of Christ, the suffering of Christ, the peace of Christ.

The article on Francis in the *Encyclopaedia Britannica* says that "probably no one in history has set himself so seriously to imitate Christ and to carry out so literally Christ's work in Christ's own way." "This," it says, "is the key to the character and spirit of St. Francis." "To neglect this point is to show an unbalanced portrait of the saint as a lover of nature, a social worker, an itinerant preacher, a lover of poverty. . . . Francis considered all nature as the mirror of God and as so many steps to God." And that's why he could call all creatures his brothers and sisters; he could sing spontaneously the Canticle of the Sun and talk to Sister Moon; he felt at home with the water and had a feeling of companionship with the birds; he could feed brother wolf when that villain was scourging the countryside; he could beg pardon from "Brother Ass, the body," for having to build it and tame it through penance. For, said he, "A man could consider himself no friend of Christ if he did not cherish those for whom Christ died," and cherish all those creatures among which Christ became incarnate.

The beautiful town of Assisi, with its stone houses and narrow winding streets, opens to unforgettable vistas. It was the home of Pietro Bernadone and his wife, to whom Francis was born in 1181 or 82 and christened John while his father was on a business trip to France. The trip was so successful that Pietro when he returned changed his son's name to Francisco, "the little Frenchman." In an age of chivalry the young Francis had a lot going for him. The Dark Ages were rapidly receding into the mists of antiquity; Christianity was blooming through an epoch of romance and fantasy. Well born, good-looking, generous and a dreamer, Francis participated in the sometimes deadly skirmishes between his and the neighboring towns. Assisi and Perugia (about sixteen miles distant from each other) fought it out in 1202 and Francis, the knight-soldier, was held prisoner for a year, after which he fell

seriously ill. The illness, like that of Ignatius, may have
been the Divine catalyst to his sanctity. A variety of
well-known incidents punctuated the process of his conversion. One form of self-confrontation came with his
casting off the common fear and nausea aroused at that
time by leprosy. That followed his noticeable lapses
into periods of silence just after he had been chosen
Master of the Revels. His companions had thought he
was in love. "You are right," he said to one friend, "I
am in love, in love with Lady Poverty."

Francis confided to another about a voice he heard
in a dream telling him that he should serve Christ in all
creatures; thus the leper whom he met begging, to
whom he gave his money, and from whom he received
the kiss of peace. It was the same voice that told him to
rebuild the church. That order he had interpreted so
literally that he sold bales of his father's wool to rebuild
the Church of San Damiano. For that the father had
him imprisoned, put in chains in fact. Francis restored
his father's property and when he was set free by his
mother rebuilt the little church with his own hands, carrying the stones to it from a distance. Indeed, he eventually restored three churches, San Damiano, San Pietro and the Portiuncula. In the process he discovered
that the way to build a church is not simply to give the
money for it; it is to give one's self to the task.

The spirit of poverty, chastity and obedience which
Francis now so visibly practiced, he had developed
through his own secret and prayerful contact with
Christ. A small group followed him, listened to him,
became enflamed with his faith and his message. Like
Augustine, he went directly to the Gospels for counsel
and, like Augustine, he stayed with and felt with the
Church. That is part of his lesson for our time.

When the hippie cult was attracting so much attention, there were serious people who saw an element of Franciscanism in some of the young men and women who were withdrawing from, or rejecting, the establishment by their unconventional clothes, hair styles and their flight from suburbia. There is no doubt that Francis' way of living after his conversion was in some respects a more dramatic departure from the lifestyle of his own kind of people than the hippies' from theirs. He, too, rid himself of his knightly gear, got rid of his clothes and went literally begging, preferring even the scraps he got from the poor and wealthy alike. But it was his interiority, his sense of direction, the evolution of a character formed on that of Christ; it was these things that made Francis different. When the Haight-Ashbury section of San Francisco was taken over by the hippies a priest friend and myself had an opportunity of viewing their situation first-hand. I talked to many of the young people themselves, to psychiatrists, social workers, police and priests who were familiar with their modes of thought and life. Regretably, I discovered, only a very small minority could claim any element of authentic Franciscanism. Regrettably, too, none of us, including the real Franciscan priests and brothers, seemed to have the grace, the inspiration or the influence to attract any of those young people to the real Francis. Indeed, tragically, too many of the Franciscan Community, like so many of all our communities, were themselves joining the dropouts.

At any rate, Francis' appeal was so essentially Christian and extended to so many people that within his own lifetime thousands joined his ever-growing community. Within twenty-five years after his death Franciscan houses spanned Christendom from Ireland to the Holy Land. The Franciscan habit was worn by king and pauper. The Franciscanism of Francis himself was as simple and unstructured as the Christianity of Christ. But it was not its structurelessness that reconverted Europe to Christ. It was its supernaturalness.

For, regardless how we theologize about the supernatural, men are made for it and restless for it.

Personally, I have a supreme distaste for the self-righteous Christian, priest or layman, who stands back from our younger generation and condemns its "misguided, shallow feelings" about love. We had become entirely too formalistic, too rationalistic, too intellectualistic; we tended to theorize and, sometimes, substitute law for mystery. I believe that, in God's providence, we (I mean we as the Church) had to experience a real shaking up to bring us back to the spirit of the Gospels. That's what Francis did for the Church of his time. We can do it too. We can do it not by sterile liberal-conservative polemics, but by thinking and feeling with Christ and His Church; by a spirit of Christian simplicity, humility and love that, like that of Francis, will find a joy, a peace, an at-homeness in everything— even suffering—that God gives or permits us.

Gentle and compassionate as Francis was, when he spoke on the need for love and poverty of spirit he "terrified" the smug and insensitive, those who set themselves up to be their brothers' judges. "Be not judges, be reconcilers," he said, "not dividers, but unifiers."

That was the way of Francis; it was the way of Christ; it can, it must be, our way.

8. Thomas Aquinas
c. 1225 - 1274
(Feast Day: March 7th)

None of his biographers quite captured the human side of St. Thomas Aquinas like Chesterton. All the warmth, imagination, luminosity, historical sense and authentic holiness of G. K. himself come into play in his unique treatment of the Dumb Ox. Aquinas needed a Chesterton for, despite his massive learning and his gigantic output of what we have traditionally referred to as his philosophy and theology, Thomas was far from being a self-revealing man. He was by vocation a searcher, an expositor, a liver of truth: truth as revealed by God; truth as discoverable through man's humble search and surrender; truth as connoted by man's life-long process of self-discovery and self-transcendence; truth as assimilated through man's union with Christ. It is significant that in Aquinas' one reference to himself, to his personal capacity for cutting through the sophistries of his time, he was more concerned with the confusion that erroneous theological theories would cause young, untrained minds than he was with winning a point or even making his own position known. The brilliant, rebellious secular cleric, Siger of Brabant, who was to be subsequently stabbed by his own mad secretary, provoked Thomas' challenge: "If he, boasting his supposed wisdom, wants to refute what we have written, let him not do it before children who are over-powered by such subtle subjects. Let him come out in the open where he will find me confronting him—and not only unworthy me, but many another whose study is Truth."

Of distinguished family background, Aquinas combined subtle intellect, massive erudition, tireless work, true humility, holiness and an enduring determination to transfuse the currently accumulated data of human thought with the spirit of Christian faith. Almost since the days of that well-known Norman adventurer, Robert Guiscard, a direct antecedent of Thomas, his family lived in a feudal castle overlooking the village of Aquino, from which they took their name; they were among Italy's noblest. Thomas himself was a grand-nephew of the Emperor Frederick Barbarossa, a blood relative of Louis of France, and kinsman to a whole contingent of self-conscious noblemen who, because of their location between Naples and Rome, were caught in the endless conflicts of Pope and Emperor. One of Thomas' brothers was executed for allegedly taking part in the overthrow of Frederick II (by the Council of Lyons); after the Council's action the entire Aquinas family had to take refuge in the papal states.

Thomas, the family's youngest son, was sent to the monastery of Monte Casino, not merely for a Christian education, but in the expectation that he would eventually become the monastery's powerful abbot. But after Frederick II's excommunication (by Gregory IX) the foreign monks, including Thomas, were chased out of Monte Casino and subsequently sent to one of the two Benedictine houses in Naples where they attended its imperial, somewhat anti-papal, university. In Naples Thomas came under the influence of Peter of Ireland and it was, partially, through Peter that he made his first contact with Aristotle, whose philosophy had been seeping in many forms through Europe, especially through the commentaries of Avicenna, Averroes, and their brilliant Spanish-Arab compatriots. It was also while in Naples that Thomas decided to leave the Benedictines and become a Mendicant friar with the newly formed Dominicans, through whom he could devote his life to the poor, to study and to prayer.

We cannot appreciate the shock Thomas caused his typically worldly family by becoming a Mendicant. Not only was their hope of a powerful abbot in the family ended overnight; the whole Mendicant movement had less respect with families like those of Aquinas than our own earlier hippies had with the Birchers or ourselves. Aquinas' mother, hearing of her son's elopement to the Dominicans, set out for Naples and from there to Rome, only to find that Thomas was on his way to the Dominican Chapter in Bologna. (Thomas would, normally, have had his full novitiate in Naples, but the Friars there had learned to expect trouble from families like his.) She then sent Rinaldo, his subsequently executed soldier brother, to kidnap him. Thomas was apprehended en route to Bologna, brought back and ensconced—some would say "imprisoned"— in his native castle, from which, after a year of futile conditioning by his ambitious mother (and his defense by a couple of sisters, one of whom became a nun), he returned to the Dominican house in Naples and was sent to Paris and Cologne. It was in one of those cities he met Albert the Great who, recognizing his genius and sanctity, became his mentor and life-long friend.

For four years (1248-52) Thomas worked as Albert's student and assistant (bachelor). During that time he was ordained to the priesthood and wrote several commentaries on Albert's work as well as on individual books and sections of the Scriptures.

In the fall of 1252 a vacancy occurred in the University of Paris where, on the recommendation of Albert, Aquinas was sent as a lecturer and doctoral candidate. Appointed also as Regent of the Dominican house in Paris, he conducted classes there but ran into problems at the university that would have driven out and broken the heart of a lesser man. The vicious hostilities between secular, monkish and Mendicant clerics were only part of the factional skulduggery that the quiet, modest and brilliant young lecturer encountered in the thriving university. After two direct interventions by Pope Alexander IV he was able to deliver his inaugural lecture; even then he and his students had to be protected by soldiers of the saintly Louis IX. Alexander's final mandate, "Receive fully and forthwith into the university community Thomas of Aquino and Bonaventure of the Friars Minor," was followed by the formal ceremony of installation which took place in the Franciscan house; it was marked by the absence of the bishop and most of his secular clergy, who were locked in mortal conflict with the Friars.

Thomas was a huge, quiet, reflective, modest and warm man whose days and hours in Paris were filled with work, writing and counselling. A biographer tells us that his morning lectures on the Bible were followed by afternoons dedicated to the current disputed questions; his evenings were spent on sermons to the clerics in the Dominican house and culminated in hours of dictation and prayer.

Among his outstanding works during his first professorship at Paris was his thesis on truth. In it he showed an extraordinary knowledge of source material and a great ability to undergird the traditional, but somewhat idealized, Platonic-Augustinian approach to theology with the realism of an Aristotle in whose reasoning Albert and himself saw great possibilities for an eventual Christian philosophic synthesis. Aquinas was, of course, a most ardent student of the great Augustine; it was the Augustinian-Platonic preoccupation with the realm of the spirit and its deprecation of the world of sense that he felt called to balance.

After his regency in Paris, Aquinas attended the Dominican Chapter (1296) in Valenciennes (midway between Paris and Cologne) and from there he returned to Italy where he taught in several Dominican colleges, acted as adviser to a couple of the popes and was made Preacher-General of the Italian Province. While in Italy he wrote his famous Summa Contra Gentiles, to assist Spanish missionaries in their theological debates with cultivated Mohammedans and Jews or, as he himself put it, to express "within the limits of my capacity the truth of the Catholic faith by the refutation of errors opposed to it." He also wrote commentaries on the Gospels and did a great deal of research on Greek Patristics after he had some Greek scholar friends make special translations of some of the Greek Fathers as well as of Aristotle. He was preparing for his future writings, including his Summa Theologiae, and his second professorship in Paris (1269-1272).

The Paris of the late sixties and seventies was even more contentious than it was during Thomas' first lectureship there. The secular-Mendicant bitterness was increasingly enflamed by charge and counter-charge. Aristotle's philosophy was known primarily through the Averroist orientation and was, therefore, suspect, and Thomas' determination to introduce an Aristotelianism (freed from Averroism) met with hostility, even from Bonaventure and the Franciscans. The Archbishop of

Paris, Ettienne Tempier, drew up and condemned a long list of Averroistic propositions and, though Aquinas was not mentioned by name, his whole philosophic approach was suspect. But, a consummate and modest intellectual steeped in faith, prayer and a love for the Church, Thomas was undaunted. He refuted with voice and pen every attempt to crush the Friars or censure the developing Christian-Aristotelian metaphysic, which was to become, through him, the philosophic substructure of Scholasticism.

Thomas' small book on the perfection of the Spiritual Life was then the most popular challenge to the attacks on the Mendicants; his tract on "The Eternity of the World Against the Murmurers," the self-proclaimed guardians of orthodoxy, the ones who "speak as though they alone were rational beings," was a reasoned and devastating blow to those unwilling to listen to the insights of a great Christian innovator.

But Aquinas' polemical writings were but a minute part of his work. He literally left no disputed subject untouched, and what Johnson said of Goldsmith applied most aptly to the Angelic Doctor: "He touched nothing that he did not adorn."

Thomas left Paris in April of 1272 and attended a General Chapter of his Order in Florence where he was designated to erect a Studium Generale for his Community in Naples (he had done similar work in the German-French Province). In Naples he lectured on Aristotle, preached the 1273 Lenten Cycle, and continued with his Summa Theologiae, stopping suddenly at the tract on Penance. He was forty-seven, worn out and beginning to slow down.

On December 6th, the Feast of St. Nicholas, 1273, he "hung up his writing instruments." After his Mass in St. Nicholas Chapel "he never wrote or dictated anything again;" the words are those of his friend and biographer, Bartholomew of Lucca. One can almost see Bartholomew's face drop as he tells of Thomas' Divine silence and surrender. When a secretary and companion, Raymond, asked Aquinas why he had given up, the saint's reply was simple and direct, "I cannot go on. All that I have written seems but mere dross when compared with what has been revealed to me." The end was not far away. Thomas was called to the Second Council of Lyons, where a last great attempt would be made to reconcile the Latins and Greeks. He left Naples for the long journey to France only to fall ill near the Via Appia. As he lay dying he asked to be taken to a Trappist monastery. His last words were a prayer of faith in and love for the Eucharistic Christ and his submission of all he ever wrote to the teaching authority of the Church. He passed in peace. Indeed, his supremely fruitful, often stormy, life had an inner peace that was never once compromised.

Though controversy still raged around his theories, the University of Paris requested his body. It was that great theology school's first tribute to its greatest scholar and saint.

Only last night I was at a party in which an internationally known choreographer, when asked to sing a song, chose the *Adoro te Devote*. As he sang the "Visu sim beatus" I could see a tear silently fall down his cheek. A convert to the Church, he told me later that he had been almost traumatized by some of the recent changes in it, but had come to Catholicism through Aquinas, and it was his sensitivity to the dynamic and innovative character of Aquinas that now stilled his fears, brought back his courage and made him newly aware that the Spirit of Christ is ever in and with His Church. This morning I told my dear old friend, Father

Martin D'Arcy, of last night's experience; Father Martin, Aquinas-like, and himself one of the great Thomists, simply said, "Praise be to God, Aquinas can never die. A great innovator, a great traditionalist, a great saint—and a model for our own turmoil-laden day."

9. Elizabeth Seton
1774 - 1821
(Feast Day: January 4)

It was Pope John who described Elizabeth Seton as an authentic American saint. She was indeed American all the way. Of British, French Hugenot and Irish stock, she grew up during the American Revolution in a family that had close personal ties with some of the great figures on both the British and American sides. Dr. Richard Bayley, Elizabeth's father, spent a two-year hitch as a naval officer in the British army, but left it to take care of his family and resume his long relationship with the Jays, the Hamiltons and the other conservative revolutionaries who were laying the foundation stones of the U.S.

Elizabeth Bayley Seton is certainly as American as they come, but she is more than American. She is an unforgettable fusion of humanness and sanctity. Emerging full-blown from the shadows of the early 1800's, she impinges on our consciousness like an intimate contemporary, one of our most personable friends. Nothing vague, concealed, plaster-cast or superficial about her. She is every bit a woman. A slim, petite, dark-eyed brunette, she has such a depth of sensitivity, affection, passion and love that one is forced to identify her with what is best, most beautiful and most lovable in one's favorite woman, one's mother, wife, daughter, friend or fiancee.

It was only when I came in contact with Elizabeth Seton's more extensive biographies, saw her in the complexities of her personal life, background and relationships, peered into her through her letters, her journals, her reflections, her prayers and her off-side comments, it was only then I became aware of how extraordinarily well she combines the most vivid qualities of femininity and sainthood. Indeed, if I were asked at this moment in which saint I find the most nuanced humanness, disciplined and consecrated by an abiding sense of God's presence, I would select Elizabeth Bayley Seton. Her native brilliance, her rich imagination, her ease of self-revelation, her inclination and her powers to express herself, all combine to form a kind of living portrait of a saint with whom any one of us could identify. As a mere child she had an aliveness, a deep sense of loneliness, a love of nature, a warmth and friendliness, a compassion. She moved from insuppressable enthusiasm to passing forms of melancholy, the latter, on one or two occasions, almost bordering on despair. But she never lost that profound sensitivity to God's presence, that total loving trust, that consciousness of the transience of human life and the imminence of death that she was to exemplify in a thousand different ways as she faced the loss of friends, the deaths of loved ones and all the tragedies which were to dog her days.

Elizabeth's mother died when she was only three years of age; in that same year her grandfather passed away in his rectory on Staten Island, leaving Elizabeth and her two sisters one-third of his estate. Dr. Bayley, her father, spent four of the eight years of his first marriage away in London developing his medical and surgical techniques. A year after the death of his first wife he married Charlotte Barclay. Charlotte taught Elizabeth her prayers, especially the Twenty-third Psalm, which was her life-long favorite, but she never was a real mother to Elizabeth; even when little Kit, Elizabeth's sister, only two years of age, was lying in her coffin, Elizabeth expressed the wish "to go to Heaven to be with Mom."

With the feeling of being unwanted in their new mother's New York home, Elizabeth and her surviving sister spent long periods of time on her Uncle William's New Rochelle farm, a 250-acre shorefront ranch overlooking Long Island Sound. William, his wife and seven children loved their little nieces and cousins; there they learned to speak French fluently, there Elizabeth became one with nature, consumed by the beauty of "every little leaf and flower, every animal and insect, by the shadows of the clouds and the waving of the trees. They were all," she said, "objects of unconnected thoughts of God in Heaven." It was there, too, Elizabeth cultivated older people, assimilating their compassion, their trust in God and their hope in heaven.

Elizabeth returned to her father's home in New York when she was eight years of age, and in the noisy enthusiasm of that post-revolutionary city she instinctively identified with her half-brothers and half-sisters, Dr. Bayley's second family, which was to eventually number seven children. He was practicing at this time with Dr. Charlton, Elizabeth's uncle on her mother's side; he also ran an anatomical laboratory in the New York Hospital, the scene of the famous Doctors' Riot when a mob attacked the hospital because it was suspected (wrongfully) the corpses with which Dr. Bayley was experimenting were stolen by body snatchers from the local cemetery. After the riot he set off for England again, leaving his second wife to take care of her own seven children, and Elizabeth and her sister Mary back in New Rochelle.

Elizabeth, more attached to her father than anyone, suffered grievous bouts of loneliness during his absence. She was certain he had abandoned her and did not love her. But, characteristic of her whole life, she retained her love for him, a love that was to become so intense that his death was one of her most agonizing losses. Dr. Bayley returned to New York in 1789 and was present at the wedding of his daughter, Mary, Elizabeth's older sister, to Dr. Post. He took Elizabeth from New Rochelle once again, back home to New York where she spent four excruciatingly miserable years. "I could not understand," she said, "why when I spoke kindly to my relations they did not speak back to me."

It was plain to her now that she would never be wanted at home; so she accepted hospitality from friends and relatives, but during those lonely, bitter years she formed several lifelong friendships; Julia Scott, Elizabeth Sadler, Catherine Duplix and, above all, William Magee Seton, that handsome, mature, well-bred, well-off young businessman with whom she danced, went to the theatre, whom she courted and finally married when she was eighteen and he was twenty-four.

At his marriage William Seton was a promising, socially acceptable, successful businessman and humanitarian. Trained in European schools, he toured and spent time in the port cities where boats of his father's shipping concern did business. He and Elizabeth had four or five years of idyllic matrimony. They loved each other intensely, they had a community of outside interests, religious, charitable and patriotic (he was chairman of President Washington's 1797 birthday ball, while she was founder-secretary of one of New York's best-known charitable organizations, a society to help poor widows). William's father had a deep attachment to his son's wife and she to her husband's seven brothers and sisters. The marriage was enriched and solidified by the births each year of their five children: Anna Maria, Rebecca, Bill, Dick and little Kit.

But their happiness was not to last. Mr. Seton, Sr. died. His successful shipping firm, which passed on to his son, suffered blow by blow from the changed political situation in New York, from piracy on the open seas and from the then current depression, necessitating his declaring a state of bankruptcy. The final stroke came for the ambitious and able young executive when he began to crumble under the family disease of tuberculosis. Elizabeth's father, for whom her affection continued to grow, had now separated from his second wife; he had his own home and had become New York's first Health Officer. But his brilliant insights into the conditions in which the awful diseases of that period, cholera, smallpox and yellow fever, flourished were no guarantee of his own protection from them. He gave himself freely to New York's hundreds of impoverished, disease-ridden immigrants, and finally got caught himself in an agonizing attack of yellow fever, to which he succumbed. Elizabeth's natural optimism, combined with her spiritual sensitivity, gave her strength to go on.

Elizabeth was a member of Holy Trinity Episcopal Church, as were her family, relatives and in-laws. Deeply religious, she followed the practices of her

Church and became attached to its priests. Dr. Henry Hobert was a particular favorite who helped her immeasurably in her spiritual life, a life which she continued to nurture amidst all her crosses. But, through a series of apparent coincidences, one of her peak spiritual experiences took place not under Episcopal auspices, but while she was attending Mass in the Madonna of Graces Shrine in Montenero, Italy. At the elevation of the Sacred Host a young non-Catholic visitor from England whispered loudly and somewhat cynically: "This is what they call the Real Presence." "My very heart trembled with sorrow and shame," she wrote, "for his rude and unfeeling interruption of their sacred adoration. I bent away from him towards the pavement, and with tears streaming down my cheek I recalled the words of Paul, 'They discern not the Lord's body.' "

Elizabeth's visit to Italy began October 2nd, 1803 when she and her sick husband and her eight-year-old daughter Anna boarded the *Shepherdess* in New York harbor, arriving in Leghorn on November 18th. In the depths of his illness, William wanted his wife to meet one of the families whose kindness, warmth and love he could never forget. They had been business connections of his father, the Filicchi family of Leghorn. William felt that they would renew in him some of the courage of his youth and would be a source of strength to his wife and daughter. When the Seton ship arrived at Leghorn the port authorities had just learned of the yellow fever epidemic in New York. They placed the family under quarantine in a small, wind-swept room without any comforts or conveniences; all the dying William had to rest on was a cold bench. Little Anna had to skip on the rope she took from around her luggage to keep warm, while her mother could do nothing but pray and be present to take care of her dying husband. The Filicchi family brought bedding and food to their stricken friends; they were unforgettable models of selfless Christian love. Through their influence the quarantine was lifted ten days ahead of time.

"It was eleven o'clock when two men carried my William to the Filicchi's carriage while I held his hand. A crowd was watching compassionately, repeating over and over, 'Oh the poor man,' " thus Elizabeth described her husband's release from the quarantine hut. In the beautiful lodging reserved for them by the Filicchis William recovered sufficiently to bring extraordinary inspiration and the consoling image of a serene death to his wife and daughter. At "a quarter past seven on Tuesday morning his soul was released," Elizabeth wrote. "I had done all that the tenderest love and the duty of a wife could do. My head had not rested for an entire week. For three days and three nights the fatigue was incessant." William was thirty-five when he died, his wife twenty-nine.

Elizabeth kept a detailed diary for her sister-in-law Rebecca of everything that happened to herself, William and her child Anna when she was in Italy. In it she revealed how the love and attention of the Filicchi family affected her. Their rich devotional and liturgical life, and the tangible comfort and strength they got from their religion aroused her interest in Catholicism and brought her into a gradual re-evaluation of her Episcopal training. Anthony Filicchi, who accompanied herself and her daughter back to New York, supplied her with biographies of the Fathers of the Church, Butler's *Lives of the Saints* and a number of catechetical and devotional manuals. Anthony, his wife and family were to remain her life-long friends. They were so close to her that she reveals in one of her letters how she had to discipline herself against allowing her friendship with Anthony to take on a too emotional character.

The Catholics of New York in Elizabeth's time were poor, rejected and unacceptable in her society. They were considered lazy, shiftless and violent. Despite the New Yorkers' intelligence, they were pathetically provincial minded; they had little idea of the history or universality of the Roman Catholic Church, little realization of their own prejudicial and enslaving mindset which made them identify poverty and illiteracy with Catholicism. The fact, for example, that Charles Carroll of Carrollton was a financier of the American Revolution and a Catholic did not occur to them; Catholicism was simply a way of life they found intolerable. Elizabeth herself had been infected with this kind of thinking, but she had discovered in Catholicism a unique way to God. Returning to New York she was already a convert at heart and felt responsible before God to further explore the Church. So conflict with the family she loved and needed was inevitable. Only a few friends showed any understanding of her mental and spiritual turmoil at this time.

She was, practically speaking, ostracized; indeed, some of her family felt that she was a victim of emotional derangement. The Rev. Mr. Hobert, her erstwhile spiritual adviser, struggled to convince her that she was acting precipitously and irrationally under the influence of the Italian Catholics who had befriended her in her grief. He gave her some literature to demonstrate what he felt was the untenability of Catholicism and, finally, like the majority of her other friends and former counsellors, he turned against her. Young Rebecca, her husband's sister, and her "soul companion," the girl for whom she had written her Italian journal, developed tuberculosis and died. Cecilia, another of her husband's sisters who was attached to her, fell seriously ill and confided that she too wanted to become a Catholic. When the family heard about Cecilia they locked her in her room and told her she would be disowned if she did not change her mind. Conditions became so inhospitable for Elizabeth that the Filicchis advised her to go back to Italy with her family, but she decided that she should remain at home and make a living for her children. One thing: her trust in God never faltered.

With the help of an old Seton associate, Elizabeth procured a small house which she turned into a boarding school for young students. There she began to make a home for her own children and there, too, began her first little religious community, the boarders and her own youngsters with whom she sang hymns and played the piano nightly.

St. Peter's in Barclay Street was the only Catholic church in New York. Its poverty, like that of its worshippers, was poignantly visible with its dirt floor, its roughly carpentered pews, its crudely painted Stations of the Cross. It was, humanly speaking, the one house of worship where you would never expect to find the Bayleys or the Setons. But for Elizabeth, with her consuming belief in the Real Presence of Christ in the Mass and the Blessed Sacrament, St. Peter's was the only church to which she felt she should go. The Filicchi family had introduced her to some Sulpician priests with whom she kept up a constant correspondence; they advised her to go to St. Peter's. On her own she had been stealing into the little church and it was there she made her Profession of Faith before Father Matthew O'Brien, its pastor's brother, March 4th, 1805. Anthony Filicchi was present for her reception into the Church and, in a letter to his wife, Elizabeth described her great joy as she professed the Faith, made a general

Confession and received Holy Communion as a Catholic.

In 1806, while at Mass in St. Peter's, Elizabeth met Father Dubourg of St. Mary's College, Baltimore. He invited her to the rectory for breakfast, and in the course of their conversation they came up with the idea of her starting a Catholic girls' school. There was no school for Catholic girls in the United States at that time; such a school would not only supply an obvious educational need, it could be a step closer for Elizabeth to religious community life, for which she had yearned ever since she left Italy. She had been already toying with the idea of a teaching job in a religious community in Montreal through which she could help with the education of her girls, send her boys to the Sulpicians and get acquainted with the Sisters. Father Dubourg's proposal must have seemed a clear answer to her prayers.

After a lot of delays and frustrations, Elizabeth set out for Baltimore where, adjacent to the college chapel, she set up her little school, her first assistant being Cecilia O'Conway from Philadelphia, who had contemplated going to Europe to join a religious community, there being no religious novitiate in the United States. Cecilia was followed by several others, including a lady who, like Elizabeth, had been married and who after her husband's death became interested in the religious life. The community soon grew beyond the capacity of its little Baltimore house; the school was filled with children and its teachers were reaching out to all the youngsters in the neighborhood and beyond.

A Mr. Cooper, who had come to St. Mary's as a late vocation candidate for the priesthood, offered ten thousand dollars to establish a house for the teaching of orphan children. It was such a godsend for Elizabeth that she considered it one of the many miracles through which God had made His will known to her as child, daughter, debutante, wife, mother, teacher, and now religious and foundress. A fifty-acre farm was purchased close to the village of Emmitsburg, fifty miles west of Baltimore; it was adjacent to Mount St. Mary's School, newly opened by the Sulpicians. A lot of preparation went into the community's transfer to Emmitsburg, as well as to the development of its first modest house and grounds; it is difficult for us to imagine how primitive were the transport and housing conditions of those days.

Before leaving Baltimore in 1808 Elizabeth made vows privately before Archbishop John Carroll, to whom she was first introduced by Anthony Filicchi on her return to the United States, and with whom she had kept in constant contact. Meanwhile, Cecilia Seton, who had now converted to Catholicism, and her sister Harriet, had joined her for the trek to Emmitsburg. Harriet was received into the Church in Emmitsburg and died there in December 1809; her death was followed by that of Cecilia who passed away in April 1810. Their heartbreaking deaths were but stations of Mother Seton's personal calvary; a calvary from which the joy of the resurrection was never more than moments away.

The Emmitsburg community grew rapidly in numbers, its members living joyfully and lovingly the kinds of hardships we associate with the Third World of our own day. They washed their homemade clothes (the community habit was patterned on one Elizabeth had seen in Italy) on the riverbank; their tiny rooms were cold and drafty, they were constantly exposed to the rain as they walked their uncultivated but scenic grounds. They were not only pioneers in formal education; they were ecologists; they developed a natural environment; they planted trees, flowers and vegetables. The War of 1812 brought their community its own kind of hardships, and there were terrible misunderstandings between the sisters and some of their Sulpician directors. In the midst of all, sickness, disease and death stalked among them. Her daughters, cousins, friends and the sisters for whom Elizabeth had such extraordinary affection were, one by one, called away in death. Her little daughter, Anna, for whom she had an intense love, a girl of rare beauty, died during her novitiate on March 12th, 1812; she was permitted to pronounce her vows on her deathbed.

It was in July of the following year that Mother Seton and her sisters made their formal vows. Arrangements had been made for her community to affiliate with the Daughters of Charity of St. Vincent de Paul. Three sisters were to come from France to train the community in the Vincentian tradition, but they were, according to one report, prevented by Napoleon from emigrating to the States. The Emmitsburg community did eventually adopt the Vincentian rule, meanwhile developing its own traditions and providing for its local needs, including Mother Seton's personal responsibility to her family. She was, of course, the community's first superior and headmistress of the St. Joseph's boarding and day schools which she and her sisters began with three neighborhood children in 1810. She had expressed her willingness several times to turn her duties over to the other sisters, but they saw in her qualities that were sorely needed for the survival of their infant community and its projects. One of these qualities was her ability to sell herself and her work. She not only influenced them spiritually, but was always able to secure material help from both her Catholic and non-Catholic friends. And, though humble, agreeable and prayerful, she did not shrink from defending the autonomy of her community from the arbitrary interference of one or two of its spiritual directors who, like so many priests since their time, did not know how to deal with women.

Mrs. Seton was a great teacher and tireless worker, as well as promoter, administrator and spiritual counsellor. Simple, lucid and convincing, her own profound spiritual convictions and her love for Christ came through everything she did, every word she spoke and wrote. And, indeed, she needed all her extraordinary qualities to keep her going. For apart from her major sufferings, her unusual background, the pioneering character of her work and that of the people (including the priests) with whom she was dealing, were occasions of endless agitations. So while she had great moments of joy as her community grew in wisdom and numbers, the cross loomed long and large on her horizon.

Four years after Anna's death Elizabeth's fourteen-year-old daughter Rebecca ("little Becky") died. She was an unusually reflective youngster and suffered a great deal. Injured while sliding on ice, she concealed her pain until a tumor formed on her thigh. "My soul's little daughter," wrote Elizabeth, "your mother's eyes fill with the thought of you still, confined to your bed, your poor little legs bandaged so tightly . . . We'll understand later how good our Lord has been to us in offering us His own Crown of Thorns." On the day of Rebecca's death Elizabeth wrote to her son William in Leghorn, "Your letter arrived while she was in her last agony, but I was able to read to her your tender expressions of brotherly love."

During all her griefs Elizabeth kept contact with Julia Scott, Elizabeth Sadler, Catherine Duplix—they were among her oldest and most loyal friends. She had known for a long time, too, that she herself was carrying the tubercular germs that wracked her family. "Eternity seems to be so near," she told Julia Scott, "it will be a beautiful, endless day for all of us." The thought of dying in the Church was a constant joy to her, as were her love for the Church, her closeness to the Blessed Mother and her devotion to our Lord in the Blessed Sacrament. Her last moments came on January 4th, 1821. "I have received Holy Communion," she exclaimed joyfully; and to the sisters who were kneeling by her bed she repeated, "Be children of the Church, children of the Church." She died with the name of Jesus on her lips.

Mrs. Seton's foundations included the first Catholic school for girls in the United States, its first native religious community and first parochial school. Her sisters who now number thousands are running hospitals, nursing schools, colleges, grade and high schools, orphanages, homes for the aged and for retarded children. Three of her own children survived her. William, whose health was a constant worry to her, lived to be seventy-two. Her second son, Richard, a United States naval officer, died in Liberia at the age of twenty-five, and her daughter, Catherine, a Sister of Mercy, lived to be ninety-one.

Elizabeth Seton was canonized September 14th, 1975 and her Feast Day is January 4th.

* * *

A PERSONAL NOTE. I have found it unusually difficult to condense, capture or even cope with the swift rush of events, the intensely activist-contemplative character, the sufferings, the prayers, the joys, the faith that seemed so integral to this extraordinary woman. Glancing through the printed copies of her letters, journals, meditations, reading the different versions of her life story, has had a strange, hopefully, redemptive effect on me. Elizabeth Seton encountered, absorbed death and disease in stark and desolating forms. Her words seem so often cries of anguish, joy, love, but more to the point, they speak a constant, a poignant, an almost palpable sense of God's presence. They echo a living, vibrant faith, a faith deep enough and rich enough to pull one through and beyond the bitterest sorrow, the most annihilating pain. Elizabeth Seton rings true, every bit of her. Thus, how she lived, what she did and said are uncommonly meaningful. In her one senses the human condition in its totality, in its mystery, in its transcendence. To meet her, even at this remove, is to face oneself with a question and a challenge. A question as to one's values. A challenge to face one's humanness, to make the human work, and in the process to enter one's mystery, as she entered hers. To embrace life as Christ embraced His Cross and, in Christ, to be lifted above the Cross to the resurrection, that was the Seton way.

I can't help hoping that the peculiar sense of the unmanageable which I have experienced in the Elizabeth Seton story will haunt my readers and myself until we begin to live a little of her faith.

10. John Nepomucene Neumann

1811 - 1860

(Beatified October 13, 1963)

On the surface of their lives and personalities, no two people would seem more unlike each other than Elizabeth Seton and John Neumann, but alike they were in their deep and abiding sense of God's presence, in their persevering commitment to Christ and their acceptance of His Cross, in their love for the Church, in their tireless capacity for self-giving, in their compassion, in their patience and humility. Mrs. Seton, native New Yorker, child of the upper crust, outgoing, urbane, convert to Catholicism, widow, superior and foundress of a great religious community, was a woman whose littlest movements had an unlooked-for drama about them. John Neumann, an immigrant who spoke English with a gutteral German accent, was small, mild-featured and seldom-spoken. "Here I am in Havre, boarding ship at last," he wrote in his infrequently kept journal. It was April 11th, 1836 and he had just taken his place on the Europa, an American three-master bound for New York.

John was born in what is now Czechoslovakia in the picturesque hill-ringed village of Prachatitz, seventy-five miles south of Prague. He was one of Philip and Agnes (Lebis) Neumann's five children. They were a simple, loving, devout, intelligent, industrious and reasonably well-off family. John went to the local school in Prachatitz and served Mass in St. Jakob's with one of whose curates he enjoyed an early friendship. In the scenic atmosphere of his native village Neumann developed a love for nature and the beginning of his life-long interest in birds, plants, trees, flowers and vegetables. His father would have been happy to have seen him study medicine, but his mother hoped and prayed that he would become a priest.

In preparation for his high school in Budweis, John combined some Latin classes in the priests' house with his regular studies in the village school. Fifteen miles from Prachatitz, Budweis was the local bishop's See town and home of the well-known beer as well as of pencil, tobacco and furniture plants. It was a historical town, too, with its thirteenth century convent and church, its Gothic abbey, eighteenth century town hall and museum. Young Neumann was a sensitive student with a hunger for knowledge, powers of concentration and a love for philosophy, languages and literature. Sometime during his school years in Budweis he made up his mind to become a priest and graduated to the local diocesan seminary where he spent two years, 1831-1833. He left there, apparently because of the anti-papal slant of some of the teachers, and enrolled in the school of theology at the Charles Ferdinand University of Prague where he completed his studies for the priesthood in 1835.

John's parents had looked forward to his being ordained locally, but the bishop was ill at graduation time, the Budweis diocese had an abundance of priests, and Neumann, with two fellow students, had applied to Bishop Kenrick of Philadelphia who was then appealing for German-speaking priests. John's interest in the

American missions had developed over the years; he knew that the thousands of Europeans fleeing to the States did not bring their priests with them. Besides, the Leopoldine Association, founded in Vienna in 1829 to help establish schools and churches for German immigrants in the United States, was active in Budweis and was publishing a paper with articles on the American missions, especially emphasizing the great need for priests among German immigrants. Disappointed that he could not be ordained at home, and frustrated at not hearing from Bishop Kenrick, John waited around for a few months, wrote to Bishop Dubois of New York, got all his travelling paraphernalia together, bade a quiet farewell to his native Prachatitz and journeyed north to Paris and Le Havre for the voyage to the United States.

Neumann reached New York on May 21st, 1836, with one dollar and a cent in his pocket. Though he had not heard from Bishop Dubois, that good man received him with open arms and promised to ordain him within a month. There were 150,000 Catholics in the New York diocese when Dubois came there, just ten years before John, and there were only eighteen priests and twelve churches to take care of them. A scholarly Sulpician priest, Elizabeth Seton's spiritual director and founder-professor of Mount St. Mary's, Emmitsburg, Bishop Dubois had nothing but trouble in New York with Irish nationalism, an intolerable Trustee System and a virulent anti-Catholicism. Less than a decade before Neumann was ordained there, the parishioners of old St. Patrick's Cathedral on Mott Street had to keep a 24-hour armed guard on it to save it from being burned down by nativist fanatics who thought the Pope was planning to take over the States. Men like John Neumann were a godsend to poor Dubois.

Five years before Neumann came to New York the Erie Canal had opened up that state's whole northeastern area, attracting hundreds of thousands of immigrants to its rich, undeveloped woodlands. There were 20,000 boats operating on the Canal when the young priest from Prachatitz boarded one of them to take up his mission assignment in the Buffalo-Niagara area. The bishop had asked him to stop off at Rochester on his way so he could meet some of the Germans there and see what he was getting involved with. He was warmly received by Father Bernard O'Reilly, the future Bishop of Hartford (Connecticut) and Father Prost, a pioneer Redemptorist, well known on the American missions. Already a devotee of Alphonsus Liguori, the founder of the Redemptorists, Neumann was attracted by the character, priestly zeal and mission-mindedness of Father Prost. Prost helped to prepare him for his work in Buffalo, and the young priest was to remember him and his Redemptorist Community during his own most discouraging moments.

Buffalo was a hustler's haven. Center of a land and housing boom, its dirt streets were flanked by wooden sidewalk-houses, stores, shops, sawmills and a new hotel. Carts and wagons rumbled their way through the town, picking up and delivering the hardware and produce that were so much a part of its people's lives. Plows, bear traps, picks and hammers, tools that helped to clear the trees, roll the logs, build the cabins and plant the rich, unruly soil; they were all on sale in Buffalo. It sounds romantic now, but Father Neumann's mission there was an unexpectedly hard, uncharted and frustrating one. Badly needed, he was scarcely appreciated by the rough, hardworking, thrifty, insecure, immigrant farmers who were scattered over hundreds of square miles; their only conscious object in life was to toil and save enough to be able to live like one of the local Yankees. John's far-flung parishioners wanted a priest, but they wanted to direct his every move. And though Neumann was not the type of man to compromise his priesthood in any way, he was too humble to fight for his rights.

For four years, with scarcely a moment for himself, Neumann made his way from dawn till dark through the beautiful undeveloped country around Buffalo, travelling on foot or by horse (he was a poor horseman) to the sick, the old, the weak and the needy. He established little schools for the children, to whom he had a special attachment, trained lay teachers and organized gangs of workmen to build his churches and missions. His first home was the attic of a little tavern run by a German couple. It was cramped but reasonably comfortable and the woman of the house cooked good German food. But Neumann had to leave there; the trustees gossiped about his living in a tavern and only a loft away from the couple and a young girl they had just brought from Germany. He moved in with another family whose log cabin was out in the woods; it was crowded, cold and uncomfortable, but the people were kind and he was away from the gossipers. Finally he was able to get a little rectory of his own with a small garden around it. There he cultivated plants, vegetables and herbs for the doctorless sick.

Bishop Dubois paid him a visit and his brother, Wenceslaus, came to stay with him; they were his two only contacts with the outside world. Constantly on the go, eating irregularly, with little sleep and hardly time for his prayers, he broke down physically. During his four years on the New York mission he had pined for some quiet time for private prayer and reflection. He had kept in mind his contact with the Redemptorists;

indeed, he had carried with him from home part of a short Italian biography of their founder, Alphonsus Liguori, which he had been translating into German. Unbeknownst to Father Neumann, Alphonsus was canonized in 1839; and, coincidentally, when Father Prost returned from the canonization he had a letter from John asking to join his community. It was 1840 when Neumann made his way via New York to Pittsburgh's makeshift Redemptorist novitiate located in Bayardstown, an island of smokestacks, taverns and hillside houses on the outskirts of the city. The six-room shanty-like structure was not what John expected a novitiate to be; unquiet, it had an endless stream of needy immigrants and its surroundings contrasted so dismally with the native beauty of the place he just left. But he craved with all his heart a more ordered life, which he was never destined to have here below.

The Redemptorists had four foundations in the States when Neumann joined them; they were run by four priests and a Brother who were dragged all over the place to minister to the Indians of Michigan or the Germans of Rochester, in the crowded hovels of Manhattan and the woods of northern Ohio. Neumann and his Novice Master came and went as their brothers did. John had little time for prayer or study; even if he had the time there were no books around. But there was the chapel where he spent the few hours he was home.

That first Christmas, 1840, he was suffering chills, fever and a cough; he was concerned about this; he did not want to be a burden to the Redemptorists. He got well, however, and continued his schedule, working among the scattered German communities of Pittsburgh. During the Holy Week of 1841 the Redemptorists received two new priests, and Father Prost brought Father Neumann to Baltimore. Even on his

way to Baltimore he had to stop off in New York to
help the priest in St. Nicholas. On Pentecost he was in
Rochester to take the priest's place there; in July he
found himself taking Father Pax's place in Buffalo; and
from there he must go to the Ohio woods. In this restless shuttling from place to place he became really fear-
ful he had made a terrible mistake to leave the diocesan
priesthood. Besides, he had heard rumors that Father
Prost was leaving the community; and Bishop John
Purcell, of Cincinnati, who was told the Redemptorists
were being withdrawn from the States because of the
impossibility of their living a community life, advised
him to go back into the diocesan priesthood. "I can
give you whole colonies of German Catholics who are
begging for a priest," he said. "Think it over and let
me know in the morning." Father Neumann, after a
restless night, decided he would go to Baltimore and
continue his novitiate. "But I had my share of temptations in the novitiate," he wrote afterward.

The Redemptorists had two Houses in Baltimore,
one in the city proper and one in Old Town. Old Town
was away from the noise and close to the woods on the
edge of Baltimore. It was much more serene and se-
cluded and there, under the guidance of Father Alexander, the new superior, Father Neumann began his
second year with the Redemptorists. It was now planned
that he would have no parish commitment; the other
priests were endlessly running backward and forward,
but he was left undisturbed. On January 2nd, 1842 he
commenced his preparation for Religious Profession
and on the 16th pronounced his vows and took the oath
of perseverance with the Congregation. That same
month he wrote a letter to his parents which was to be
mailed from Vienna by Father Alexander who was visiting the motherhouse there. In it he confessed to his

parents that none of their letters had ever reached him and he wondered if they received his. "Body and soul now," he wrote, "I belong to the family of St. Alphonsus. I have made my vows as a Redemptorist missionary. With the example and encouragement of my brother religious I can be a better priest. Wearing this holy habit and living this holy Rule, dear parents, I can walk without fear, even into the Valley of Death."

Archbishop Eccleston had given the Redemptorists the care of all the German Catholics in the state of Maryland, and that enormous responsibility now fell to Fathers Joseph Fey and John Neumann. They worked out of their little house in Old Town from which they could see in the distant wharves the ships from Antwerp, Bremen, Havre and Trieste that had carried thousands of German families up the Chesapeake. It's hard for us to imagine how those immigrants from Europe must have felt; poor, homesick, bedraggled, away from their own wayside shrines and from the beauty, love and stability of their history-laden cities and villages. The Catholic church in Old Town was for many the only link with all that they loved, the only familiar landmark in a new and strange world. For the two priests it was a twenty-four-hour-day mission. Catechism classes, convert instructions, Baptisms, endless problems with young people; families separated or fever-stricken, people out of work, people unable to speak the language, widows with children running away, immigrants bilked of their savings, dropping dead of heart attacks or knifed in brawls. Yet Father Neumann was to say later that his two years in Baltimore as a simple curate were the happiest of his twenty-four in the States.

In March of '44 he was told to report to Pittsburgh as superior. He longed to beg off, but he felt his vow of

life-long obedience did not permit even an expression of
what was in his mind. Pittsburgh was building a new
church and Father John was responsible for its comple-
tion; he was responsible, too, for the Germans of Pittsburgh and their brothers scattered all over Pennsylvania. Times were bad and he devised the St.
Philomena Building Association in which all the Catholic workers could enroll as members by giving a quarter
a month. Thrifty Germans could also invest in the Association. He divided the work among himself and the
other Fathers, but insisted they live a community life
where at all possible. The church was dedicated in October 1846 and by Christmas Father Neumann was in
bed with fevers and chills. He was recalled to Baltimore
and it looked as if he could have some quiet at last.

But in February of '47 John was informed by the
motherhouse in Europe that he was to take charge of
the entire Redemptorists in the United States, now
thirty men and ten foundations. The men included Aus-
trians, Frenchmen, Prussians, Hollanders, Czechs, Belgians, Alsatians and two Irishmen who had just entered
the novitiate. The letter from Belgium making Father
Neumann their superior warned him of some of the
problems. Generous donations from Austria and Ba-
varia had been spent on German-American churches,
immigrants and schools, and now these churches must
be enlarged; but the community owed more than a
quarter million dollars which would have to be collected from families receiving less than three dollars a
week. Wrestling with the requests of the motherhouse
would not be easy, but Neumann's approach was characteristic: he would transfuse each house with an increasing degree of holiness; the community prayers and
Rule which he had just translated from the Italian must
be followed meticulously.

Though combining humility and compassion with exactitude, he was criticized. One young man complained that he was "running St. Alphonsus (in Baltimore) as though it were a novitiate." But, undaunted, he went ahead, working with the community, working among the people, ministering to communities of nuns in the area. "The superior is not to seem superior or like an overlord," he wrote in a little notebook, ". . . Jesus taught the very opposite, both by word and example." He had his own kind of humor, which the brethren knew: "My two wild Irishmen (Duffy and McCrain) are now talking German as well as myself," one Father wrote him when asking for his translation of the Rule. And Father Neumann himself continued studying the languages of the people to whom he must minister. In a letter home he wrote, "Since we now have a House in New Orleans I have been studying Spanish." He was still criticized. "He may be a paragon of piety," one young man wrote, "[but] he has no presence." To his great joy, Neumann was replaced in January of '49 by Father Bernard Hakkenscheid. Bernard was a master linguist with a doctorate in theology. "He has the warmth that I lack," Neumann wrote, "he can break tensions anywhere with a good-natured laugh."

In his fifteen years in the States the first letter John Neumann received from 29 Upper Lane, Prachatitz, the home of his father and mother, came just after the appointment of Father Bernard. It was on St. Joseph's Day and he was thrilled to see the envelope. But it contained a rather sad reference to: "My letter of two years ago telling you of Mother's beautiful death." It was the first time he had heard of his mother's death. Like Elizabeth Seton's, his was a life punctuated with sadness.

On Easter Tuesday, 1851, Archbishop Eccleston of

Baltimore died, and that summer Archbishop Kenrick came from Philadelphia to be Ordinary of Baltimore. Kenrick was a giant of a man, physically and intellectually; he spoke German fluently with a Dublin accent. Immediately he became attracted to Neumann and selected him as his confessor. Though they were two such totally different men, their esteem for each other was mutual. Kenrick was a man of great eloquence, immense scholarship and indestructible calm in controversy. Neumann, himself brilliant, admired the archbishop, but was surprised at the archbishop's interest in him.

Word began to spread around that Neumann was to be chosen the Bishop of Philadelphia. When it came to his attention he wrote letters to Belgium, Vienna and Rome, pleading with them, and subsequently with Kenrick, that he did not want to be a bishop. He prayed fervently that the chalice would pass from him; but one day while he was away Kenrick left his own ring and pectoral cross for him, and returned later with two letters, one appointing the humble, prayerful, hard-working Redemptorist, John Nepomucene Neumann, Bishop of Philadelphia, the other demanding explicit and formal obedience to the appointment. His appointment was received with surprise and mixed feelings. Some of the Catholic upper crust in Philadelphia did not want a man with a foreign accent. They were afraid of the No-Popery people whose motto was "America for the Americans."

Bishop Neumann was consecrated March 28th, 1852 in St. Alphonsus where enormous crowds of people had gathered to felicitate him. It was April when he arrived in Logan Square, Philadelphia, and the foundations of the cathedral (which Bishop Kenrick had started in 1846) were just above the ground. Philadelphia, a history-laden, bigoted city in Neumann's time, had a strong Catholic influence, but just eight years before he went there it was the scene of nativist riots which in one instance led to the burning of St. Michael's Church and Convent, attacks on St. Augustine's, the destruction of forty dwelling houses and displacement of 200 Catholic families. In that riot sixty persons were seriously injured and fourteen lost their lives; it was followed later on in the year by another riot in which fifty persons were wounded and killed.

Bishop Neumann lived only eight years in Philadelphia, during the last four of which he received substantial help from Bishop James F. Wood, a native Philadelphian who was made his coadjutor in 1857. During Neumann's episcopacy over eighty churches were constructed in the diocese. He was the first bishop in the country to organize the parochial schools into a diocesan system and he increased the number of pupils two thousand percent. But these were only some of the visible fruits of a life that was one continuous round of personal prayer and service to the needy, the sick, the children and to the countless thousands of others for whom he was constantly available.

Following in the footsteps of Charles Borromeo, who in 1574 had the Blessed Sacrament exposed in thirty churches in Milan to atone for the sins of the city, Neumann set up the Forty Hours Devotion on a diocesan basis and went from church to church promoting devotion to Christ in the Blessed Sacrament. His yearly visitations took him into every parish and mission station of the diocese, where often he would stay for a week to meet the people and talk with them. He brought in several teaching Orders and founded his own Sisters of the Third Order of St. Francis in Philadelphia, as well as its preparatory seminary. He wrote articles for newspapers, published his famous catechism, visited his schools continuously, acted as Spiritual Director in many of the convents and lectured in pastoral theology in St. Charles Borromeo Seminary. Always interested in the languages of his people, he mastered a speaking knowledge of at least ten, including Gaelic, and encouraged the building of national churches, one of which was the first Italian church in the country. Until he went to Philadelphia, English was Neumann's auxiliary language, but he immediately made it his principal language, and while he always wrote it well, he got one of his priests to help him develop his speech so that his talks and lectures were jammed with people.

When Neumann went to Philadelphia he appealed to the trustees of Holy Trinity Church, who had been fighting with several of his predecessors, to put their appointments in the hands of the bishop. Several of the parish officials opposed him and took the case to court; the court handed down a verdict against Neumann, but he appealed to the Superior Court of Pennsylvania, meanwhile refusing to allow priests to say Mass in Holy Trinity. "If you want Divine Service in this building," he told the parishioners, "you must cede the property to the diocese." And he explained later, "We may have no alternative but to go into debt and build a second church nearby." After two years the Superior Court overruled the lower court. "Anyone who wishes to be a member of the Catholic Church," Bishop Neumann told Judge Woodward, "must be united with his pastor and, through his pastor, with the bishop and the Pope," and Judge Woodward told the trustees, "You are a disgrace to Philadelphia. From time out of mind you have been fighting with your bishops. Once you had an American, then an Irishman; now you have one of your own, a German. None has ever suited your taste . . . You cannot expect your contumaciousness to be abetted by the court." It was a landmark decision, one that helped break the heart of the Know-Nothing movement, as well as the Trustee System.

Bishop Neumann travelled to Rome to participate in the Proclamation of the Dogma of the Immaculate Conception (December 8th, 1854) and while in Europe visited his childhood home and aged father in Prachatitz. He was given a tumultuous reception by the local people and dignitaries. He dined with the ex-Emperor Ferdinand and had a long audience with Pius IX, who had a great personal admiration for himself and his work. He returned to a Philadelphia stricken with poverty; the immigrants were still coming in the thousands, the churches were trying to help needy families.

Neumann wanted his huge diocese divided; he wanted also a coadjutor. Archbishop Kenrick proposed that Philadelphia be made an archdiocese, but Neumann thought it should not; it had no cathedral. When he was given the well-bred Bishop Wood in 1857 Neumann took a small room in his house, turning everything else over to the new bishop. But he continued to work himself, even as his pace slowed and his color ashened. At three-thirty in the afternoon of January 5th, 1860, as he made his way back to his house while reciting the Rosary, he staggered forward, clutched the hitching post outside a private residence, was taken inside and died. He was given the Last Rites there by Father Quinn. After a relatively short, crowded and prayerful life, John Nepomucene Neumann, the boy from Prachatitz, made his final trip—to God. The sanctity of his life was recognized everywhere he was assigned.

On October 13th, 1963 Neumann became the first American bishop to be beatified; his canonization is awaited. How surprised he would have been.

11.   The Uganda Martyrs

Their Names, Their Backgrounds and the Way They Died

1885 and 1886

(Feast Day: June 3)

How do you react when your name is called out among a crowd of people waiting for dinner in a restaurant, in a doctor's office, among a group of applicants for a job, a degree or a political appointment? Does a printed version of your name appearing in the middle of a page attract your attention before you read what has come before it? Does the name of a schoolmate or of a deceased friend ring up any special memories for you? Names are more than mere words for, or marks made by, the persons who bear them. Primitive peoples, including the peoples of the Bible, saw the person, his nature, his character, his power in his name. The name is the person for whom it stands; at least to the extent that he is known to the one who hears or uses his name.

On October 18th, 1964 Pope Paul VI called out the names of twenty-two young Africans who were tortured, mutilated and burned alive because they had committed their lives to Christ in an atmosphere that was almost totally alien to everything Christ stood for.

The names of those young men, like some of the Biblical names, or the names of the early Christian martyrs, will look strange when you see them in print, but please read on. Get to know something about the young men themselves, something about their personalities, their courage, the circumstances of their lives and deaths. Think about them when you listen to the news from Africa, when you are shocked by the brutality of man to man, or when you wonder, really wonder, if Christianity can transform any kind of culture or personality. There were many Christians and non-Christians in the Uganda of the 1880's who suffered the same fate as its twenty-two Catholic martyrs, but the Church made a thorough investigation of the lives and backgrounds of those twenty-two and canonized them for their extraordinary heroism and Christian witness. They died between November of 1885 and June of 1886, and their Feast Day is June 3rd.

It was on June 3rd, 1886 that Charles Lwanga, chief page in the royal court of Buganda, was burned over a slow fire in the Valley of Namugongo, about sixteen miles from the palace. That day thirteen others met the same fate. Here are their names, ages and offices: Luke Banabakintu, age 30, was a regional official of the kingdom; James Buzabaliawo, age 25, was the court's assistant general bandmaster; pages of the Royal Audience Hall were Gyavira, age 17, Ambrose Kubuka, 18, Anatole Kiriggwajjo, 20, Achilles Kiwanuka, 17, Mbaga Tuzinde, 17, Mukasa Kiriwawanvu, 20, Adolphus Mukasa Ludigo, 24, Bruno Serunkuma, 30; Kizito, age 14, and Mugagga, 16, were pages of the Inner Private Courts; and Jean-Marie Muzeyi, age 30, was former page of King Mutesa I.

On November 15th, 1885 Joseph Mukasa Balikuddembe, Majordomo of the royal palace, age 25, was

beheaded and burned; on May 26th, 1886 Denis Sse-
buggwawo, royal page, age 16, met with the same fate,
and Pontian Ngondwe, 35, palace guard, was hacked to
pieces; the following day Athanasius Bazzekuketta, 20,
royal page, was hacked to death, while another page,
Gonzaga Gonza, 24, was speared and beheaded. Finally, on May 3rd, 1886, Noe Mawaggali, 35, royal potter,
was speared and savaged by dogs. The names are pronounced exactly as spelled, each vowel having equal
value.

Like all of hinterland Africa, Uganda and its people were hidden, mysterious and remote until the late
1800's, when a new nationalist-imperialist spirit gripped
Britain, France, Germany and the other European colo-
nial powers. Straddling the equator, south of the
Sudan, bordered on the west and southwest by Rwanda
and Zaire, on the east by Kenya and on the south by
Tanzania, with which it shares Lake Victoria, Uganda
was designated by an Anglo-German agreement of
1890 as being within the British sphere of influence.
The previous year Germany had made a treaty of protection with Buganda, the largest and most progressive
of the four kingdoms in Uganda. But the British-Ger-
man conference which met to allocate spheres of influence in Africa to the European powers already operating on its periphery cancelled the German treaty;
Uganda thus became and remained a British protector-
ate until 1962, when it was given its independence, its
first president being Mutesa II, King of Buganda, with
Dr. Milton Obete his prime minister. Obete retained his
office until 1971, when he was overthrown by the well-
known and flamboyant General Idi Amin.

Uganda, a richly agricultural and beautiful
country, made a life-long impression on the young Win-
ston Churchill. "The forests of Uganda," he wrote in

1908, "for magnificence, for profusion of brilliant life and awful fecundity eclipsed all [my] previous experiences." Written records of the area go back only to the time of its first European explorers. Arab traders entered the territory in 1840 to deal in ivory and slaves, the British explorer, Captain John Hanning Speke came in 1862, followed by Henry Morton Stanley in 1875, with Alexander Mackay of the Church Missionary Society of England arriving in 1877, and the White Fathers two years later.

Founded in Algiers in 1868 by Archbishop Charles M. Lavigerie, the White Fathers to a man reflected a strong measure of the heroism, the extraordinary spiritual resources, the sensitivity, the dedication and the organizing skills of their remarkable progenitor. Lavigerie taught at the Sorbonne, organized world support for the persecuted Christians in Lebanon, held one of the highest posts in the Vatican, at thirty-seven was France's youngest bishop, the Bishop of Nancy, and in 1865 was appointed to the archbishopric of Algiers. With an Arab population that was famine-ridden, infested with cholera and eaten by a plague of locusts, and with a Church kept impotent by an anti-clerical French bureaucracy, Algeria was unconsciously crying out for a man of Lavigerie's caliber. His first statement of purpose shook its officialdom to its roots: We must challenge the "blindness and impotence that we have seen for thirty years in Africa . . . the calculated absence of any Christian thought." Algeria is the "only door of Providence on a continent of 200 million souls to whom we must bring the Gospel, even at the cost of our lives." The provincial government hated him, but he scorned their opposition.

Working twenty-four hours a day, Lavigerie threw himself with Pauline zeal and resourcefulness into feeding the hungry Arabs, while sending his personal representatives all over Europe to plead their cause. When the government ordered him to surrender his Moslem orphans on the grounds that he was proselytizing them, he told them with tart definitiveness: "I would gladly return the children if they had parents; but they have none. I am their parent, the one who kept life and breath in them, and only brute force will take them from them." His policy of Africa for the Africans, his crusade to make the European nations who had officially abolished slavery in their own dominions stop the slave traders at their source, the kind of men he looked for in his missionaries, and his personal blueprint for their work, made him a prophet a century ahead of his time. He cautioned his men against trying to make converts of the Arabs. They were simply to live among them, dress like them, eat their food, nurse their sick, feed their hungry; in short, they were to reincarnate the authentic spirit of Christ wherever they went, and having once spread the Good News they were to return to their own countries. "Do not Europeanize the people," he said, "make yourselves what they are; give a Christian interpretation to their customs, their songs and dances. Be men of prayer and do not be in a hurry to succeed. Remember you are there for God."

In 1878 Lavigerie submitted to Pope Leo XIII his plan for the evangelization of Central Africa and the Pope responded by appointing him Apostolic Delegate to four enormous territories to be entrusted to his White Fathers, who then numbered less than eighteen members. In May of that same year the first caravan of ten missionaries set out from the coast of Tanganyika to the interior; they split into two groups at Tabora, four priests and a Brother (Fathers Lourdel, Livinhac, Girault and Barbot, and Brother Amans) heading for

Uganda. Mutesa I, the third reigning monarch of Buganda, was twenty-three years on the throne when the White Fathers arrived. A tall, handsome, well-built, proud, self-confident and aggressive man, he had helped to build his country at the expense of its neighboring territories into a huge, well-organized dictatorship. The unrivalled monarch of Equatorial Africa, with his standing army, his fleet of thousands of canoes, his battle-hardened warrior chiefs, his absolutist rule, combining like the ancients the roles of king and priest, he feared none, none, that is, with the exception of the greedy, armored Europeans; the Belgians and French on the north and west, the Germans on the south and the British on the east. He had the salutary example of a black rival in the Sudan who had come to prominence with Arab slavers' guns; his only desire, therefore, was to form a treaty of protection with a European power possessing the most up-to-date equipment. His primitive identification of religion and rule made it impossible for him to distinguish between a country's missionaries and its political representatives, and the then British alignment between both may have helped to mislead him on the matter.

Mutesa received the missionaries relatively well, presented them with temporary headquarters and gave them freedom to evangelize in his territory. He even offered to become a Catholic if they would make a political deal with France on his behalf. He was, of course, suspicious of white people's motives, he recognized the rivalry between the French and the English (and, tragically, between Catholics and Protestants also) and he was clear as to the basic differences between Moslem and Christian beliefs. He saw the merits of Catholicism and was sensitive to its virtues, but totally immersed in his essentially pagan folkways he simply could not allow himself to identify with the Christian way of life.

The missionaries assigned to Mutesa's territory had a startling influence on the people with whom they came into contact; their letters describe the Bugandans as intelligent and sensitive people, hungry for a disciplined and self-sacrificing way of life, and thus singularly open to Christianity. The Fathers' first house was built in July of 1879; its chapel was dedicated on the Feast of the Immaculate Conception the same year. The workers Mutesa assigned to the building, as well as the people in the area, were so advanced in their appreciation of the faith that the priests, though directed by Lavigerie to conduct a two- or three-years' catechumenate for potential converts, baptized four of the future martyrs on March 27th of 1880 and four others on May 14th the same year. They included Joseph Mukasa and Andrew Kaggawa, prominent members of the court, as well as Matthias Kalemba and Luke Banabakinto, regional officials. What the Fathers had noticed especially about their converts and catechumens was the intensity of their interest in Christ and their willingness to give up any of their cherished ways of life that conflicted with the spirit of Christ. They would surrender their wives, slaves, possessions, they were willing to serve others personally, to take care of them when they were sick, to resist taking bribes, to stay out of fights even with their enemies, to forego vengeance, to forgive, to witness to and preach Christianity, to instruct others in the faith, both overtly and secretly.

Despite his intelligence, Mutesa was a victim of the grossest superstitions; they were endemic to his culture, a part of his unconscious. He insisted, e.g., on ritual executions to placate not the supreme creator God whom his people thought to be cruelly indifferent to their lives, but to satisfy the vengeful, bloodthirsty minor spirits whose demands were endlessly diagnosed by his witch doctors and mediums. He leaned towards Islam as a religion that would be more compatible with his superstition, greed and lust. So, his people, who were becoming Christian, found themselves increasingly at variance with the barbaric customs to which he was so inured, and they kept reminding the missionaries of this. The missionaries, strong-willed men themselves, protested against some of what was going on in Mutesa's court; they did so diplomatically, but they became more and more personae non gratae. Finally, they and the catechumens, who probably numbered a couple of hundred, felt threatened by the king who was being pushed by his prime minister and witch doctors to liquidate them. They thus decided to leave Buganda and return at a more propitious time. Their founder had given them an absolute rule that they were not to expose their own lives or the lives of their catechumens to unnecessary death.

The catechetical situation in Buganda was indeed extraordinary; there were four centers of Catholic teaching there which were to become an enduring catechumenate even when the priests had gone. The royal palace with its adjoining buildings was a gigantic complex built of bamboo, elephant grass and mud; it accommodated at least three thousand people with its sleeping quarters, audience halls, conference rooms, etc. There Joseph Mukasa, the king's Majordomo, was shepherd and catechist. He was assisted by Jean-Marie Muzeyi, and later by Charles Lwanga, who were still catechumens. Andrew Kaggwa and his assistant, Matthew Kisule, carried on the apostolate of teaching in the outer enclosure. Mitwana, one of the regional headquarters, served as a catechetical center for Matthias Kalemba and Luke Banabakintu, and Kitanda in the

Bulemezi region was directed by Charles Lwanga. In the royal enclosure itself there were about a hundred and fifty adherents to the Catholic Faith in various stages of instruction. Mukasa, Mutesa's favorite and trusted attendant, kept these people on their toes as Christians. He was recognized by everyone, including the pagans and Muslims, as a man of strange integrity, anxious to care for the physical, spiritual and moral welfare of those who wanted to live the good life. He gathered the Christians together in small groups, prayed with them, instructed them in their faith and encouraged them to live lives of Christian love. The other centers were taken care of by equally heroic teachers. The missionaries' letters make many references to their "delicacy of conscience," "heroic devotion," "willingness to give up everything for Christ." "Of marriageable age and in a position to marry advantageously, Jean-Marie chooses to remain celibate," writes Father Lourdel. "Others redeem young children from slavery; their Christian service is a most visible expression of the New Life . . . How absurd to underestimate the efficacy of God's grace. The Creator of the World knows how to gather lilies where He will and does so where it is humanly impossible. He revives the courage of missionaries by the daily witness of men who rise miraculously above the depths of moral decadence that surrounds them."

The missionaries moved quietly away, much to the joy of Mutesa's prime minister. Among the men who left them at their boats on the lake was Mwanga, third son of Mutesa, who was to succeed to the throne. He regretted the Fathers had to leave and hoped they would return. They worked tirelessly on the other side of the lake, keeping secret contact with their Bugandan catechumens and returned for the accession of Mwanga to the throne in 1885. Mutesa had died in 1884. They were received with open arms by Mwanga, but they couldn't help noticing how he had changed in appearance and in mentality. Weak, giggly, self-indulgent, cruel and unpredictable, he was enmeshed in other vices, African hemp and sodomy. While he retained his father's evil-minded, greedy and demonically hostile prime minister, his most prominent appointments were given to Catholics or catechumens like Mukasa and Lwanga; indeed, the list of royal appointments read like a litany of catechumens and they continued their Christian evangelization systematically while giving the ultimate in virtuous service to their king.

But the clash was bound to come. Several things happened to provoke the frenzy of this young, intemperate and maniacal dope addict. First, he was being deprived of playing around sexually with his favorite page boys; and that was for him the most intolerable restraint. But there were other things. Although he had, like his father, a strange sensitivity to the merits of Christianity, he compulsively invoked the help of mediums, witch doctors and the satellite gods whom his prime minister kept reminding him of, especially in times of natural disasters, plagues, accidental burnings, etc. He was frightened and intimidated by the power of the white men in his court, and he was agitated beyond his capacity by a prime minister who wanted the white Christians annihilated. Every day he changed his moods, pleading with and crying to the missionaries at one time, or threatening behind their backs to have them burned to death. Father Livinhac was made a bishop and following his appointment the Missionary Church Society of England appointed a Bishop Hannington to Uganda. Hannington, who wanted to visit his missions, had the misfortune of entering the country from the north, despite the Bugandans' horrifying superstition that strangers from the north would come through and destroy their kingdom.

Mwanga, with the help of his prime minister, dispatched a group of murderers to kill Bishop Hannington and the members of his caravan. Father Lourdel and Mackay found out about this through one of the courtiers and pleaded with him to cancel his orders, but it was too late. Hannington and his entire caravan were wiped out. When he discovered that the court secrets were leaking out Mwanga became furious to the point where his animal-like passions played havoc with him. From then on the smallest incidents in the court provoked him. By accident he discovered that his favorite page boy, the son of his prime minister, was receiving instructions from Denis Sebuggawa. This was the incident that set off the holocaust in which twenty-two martyrs and dozens of others were brutally killed.

The first man to fall victim to the young king's rage was Mukasa, his trusted friend and aid. Screaming, he challenged him to know why he was trying to take his kingdom away from him; he called him a thief, a traitor and a Catholic. Mukasa told him with the utmost dignity, "I am your servant and your friend. I am not a thief or traitor, but I am a Catholic and I'm ready to die for my faith." Mwanga ordered him executed immediately. "You are to be burned alive," he told him. Mukasa was seized on by the executioners, who did not want him to suffer the horrible death of burning; he was beheaded with an axe and his body burned. The next one to fall victim to the king's anger was Charles Lwanga, now chief of the pages. He, too, was trying to protect the pages from being perverted by the king, but his death was to await their common massacre. Meanwhile Denis Sebuggawa, who admitted giving instructions to Mwafu, the prime minister's son and the king's favorite page boy, was ordered executed, but before he left his presence Mwanga took a lance from a nearby guard and broke it over his shoulders. In that berserk state he struck Mwafu on the face with all his strength, breaking his teeth, and ordered the gates locked for the night so that no Christians could get out. On his way to his sleeping quarters he came upon a young assistant to Charles Lwanga and asked him if he too were a Christian. When he answered, "Yes," Mwanga ordered him to be mutilated. Continuing on his satanic path, he met a young man receiving instructions from Mr. Mackay, and with the part of the lance he had used on Denis Sebuggawa he beat the young man on the face until blood poured from his wounds; then he kicked him into unconsciousness.

Lwanga got the page boys together and told them that to escape death they would have to give up their faith, but that was up to them, he said. With one voice they said they would be better off dead than giving up their faith. The following morning the pages were ordered to present themselves to Mwanga. Meanwhile the executioners holding Denis postponed his death, thinking he might be reprieved as he was the nephew of the prime minister. But when no word came he was stabbed with daggers in the woods and left for vultures to devour. Lourdel and Mackay tried to see Mwanga, but to no avail. He was already seeking the approbation of his chiefs for the martyrdom of the Christian pages. The chiefs, including some of the fathers of the pages, approved of the barbarities. Mwanga called them together, ordering those who prayed with the white men to step aside. He gave them a last chance to deny their faith, but they refused. Mwafu, the prime minister's son, was reprieved, a decision he himself repudiated. A protestant boy was given to a Moslem chief, but when being carried away he fought so wildly that he was beaten to death.

Older men, including soldiers, clerks and court officials who were Christians, determined to die with the youngsters they were unable to save. Andrew Kaggawa was decapitated in front of the prime minister's house. Pontain Ngondwe, the soldier, was stabbed by lances at the gates of the royal enclosure. Matthias Kalemba, a Catholic leader in the Mengo region, had his arms cut off at the elbow and his legs at the knee. With demonic exactitude, the executioners tied his arteries and veins so that he would not die too quickly. Bits of flesh were sliced from his body and roasted in front of his eyes. Noe Mawaggli, another regional chief, was tied to a tree while guards spent an hour using him for target practice. That day a hundred people died because they were Christians or suspected of being Christians, or because someone who disliked them accused them of having prayed to the Christian God.

The calmest of those destined for death were the pages. Tied together in bunches, they inched their sixteen miles' journey to Namugongo, the Valley of Death. A page on the way demanded to be killed and get it over with. He was hit by clubs and taken along. The memory of the calm, serenity and apparent joy of the pages lived for half a hundred years in the district. The young men were Christians only a short time. Several were baptized by Charles Lwanga the night they were arrested. On the night of June 2nd the drums began sounding in preparation for the burning to death of those young men the following day. They prayed and sang hymns while almost a hundred executioners in frenzied madness prepared for the holocaust, drinking, dancing and building the pyre of wood and reeds.

One of the victims was a nephew of the chief executioner. Rather than burn him to death the executioner ordered that they club him into insensitivity before wrapping him in the shroud of reeds. One by one the young men stepped forward to be wrapped in reeds and placed on the pyre. Lwanga refused to be tied up, arranged his own deathbed and stretched out upon it. On a signal from the executioner, the pyres were put in flames. There were no screams of pain, only sounds of prayer. Even the most maniacal of those standing around, including the executioners, were stunned into silence by the quiet dignity of the suffering youths. The White Fathers that morning were under virtual house arrest in order to keep them from going to the pages. They had knelt all night in prayer in the chapel. It was noon when a man arrived from Manugongo and told them how the boys seemed to have died, miraculously preserved from pain. "This is how God wanted it," Livinhac said, and led the priests back to the chapel for prayers of thanksgiving.

It was June 3rd, 1886, the Feast of the Ascension.

12. Miguel Agustin Pro

(Father Pro)

1891 - 1927

It was the evening of November 23rd, 1927, small groups of frightened looking Mexicans could be seen here and there, glancing bewilderingly at the photographs of two young brothers who had been executed by a firing squad on that morning. Taken by a government agent, the photographs were spread across the front pages of the Mexican press. The dead brothers were Miguel and Roberto Pro. Particular attention had been given to Miguel. He was photographed before he left his jail cell, while he faced the firing squad, his arms outstretched in the form of a cross, and when the chief of the execution squad was standing over his crumpled body, discharging the final shot.

Miguel Agustin Pro, or Father Pro as he was best known, is an example of heroic holiness achieved in a very complex kind of socio-political environment. He reflects in a special way, too, the poignancy, the passion and the agonizing contradictions that have been so much a part of his country's history. To know Father Pro is to know Mexico at its best. It would take volumes to give perspective to the depth and complexity of the forces that have gone into the making of Mexican history. That rugged, mineral-rich, backbone of a country with its diversity of physical and geological features, its friendly, sensitive, passionate peoples and its vast conglomerate of cultures, has had one unifying bond—religion. Both the advanced and primitive cultures which the first Spaniards encountered in what is now Mexico were essentially religious. Idolatrous and highly ceremonial, the Aztecs who dominated the central plateau engaged in human sacrifice, and to some degree in ritual cannabalism. Their priests and warriors were a distinctive caste, but as in all primitive cultures, their religion and politics merged in their rulers, and that has been Mexico's continuous destiny.

In one of those curious coincidents of history, the essential interweaving of king and Church in the Latin Americas had a background not only in their pre-Columbian past, but in Spain itself, that multi-cultural peninsula where the migrants of Phoenicia, Carthage and Rome, bound together by the Christian faith, looked to the Church to continue the assimilation, conquest or conversion of Visigoth, Moslem and Jew. The Spanish authorities played a direct and purposeful role in the Christianizing of their colonies. Evangelization was a vital part of their responsibilities and was canonized by several Church-state *(patronato real)* covenants. The Spanish government collected tithes to defray the expenses of church building and development. They presented candidates for bishoprics and other ecclesiastical offices. They issued permits for churches, monasteries, hospitals and schools, and they gave their official approval for the publication of Church documents.

Though supported by their government, the early Spanish missionaries were men of extraordinary faith, zeal and courage. They criss-crossed endless mountain ranges to Christianize seven hundred tribal groups who spoke more than a hundred languages and dialects. They studied the languages, reflected on the inner workings of the tribal mind, mastered the habits and customs of their people and interested themselves in the natural phenomena around them, as well as in Indian antiquities and arts. They taught the Indians new ways of building, new styles of design, new kinds of painting. The erection of thousands of churches in which Spanish and Indian traditions were fused and the growth of a distinctive and highly ornate style of art and architecture is vivid witness to the patient work of men who were not only priests, but teachers, psychologists, artists, scientists and anthropologists. At the close of that first era of missionary activity the Church in Mexico was not only organized into dioceses, monasteries, hospitals and welfare institutions, it was apostolically active, socially conscious and run by a zealous group of self-sacrificing concerned priests whose human models were the Apostles and Fathers of the Infant Church.

In the late 1700's there was a noticeable decline in religious fervor, both in Spain and its colonies. There was the increasing intervention of the Spanish government in the Mexican Church, the French and American revolutions, the Enlightenment with its built-in skepticism, strong anti-Church bias and Freemasonry; during this period the numbers and quality of the clergy declined. The Church grew richer. Tithes collected by the government, fees for baptisms, marriages and funerals, large gifts from private individuals meant great revenues for the Church; its holdings represented a substantial percentage of the capital of the country, an unhealthy situation. With Spain's general policy of not ordaining Indians to the priesthood, and the work of the missionaries confined to urban areas, the majority of the population remained illiterate. The Indians in the outlying areas were baptized, but they scarcely ever saw a priest, so that their Christian Faith and practice reflected their pre-colonial cults as much as those of the Catholic Church, of which they were sincere members. Many historians feel that a radical transition was taking place all through the South Americas just before their independence movements, and that had colonization continued longer the Church and Catholicism would have done much better work in social transformation. However that may be, the churchman's position in Spanish America was extremely vulnerable on the eve of its independence from Spain, and the anticlericalism of today's Mexico goes back to that period.

Fathers Hidalgo and Morales, Mexico's first political insurrectionaries, wanted to preserve the privileged position of the Church while initiating radical social reforms, and the combination of wealthy Spanish and Creoles who actually achieved independence in 1821 were determined to keep the country officially Catholic. But Catholicism was not pervasive enough to undergird a politically cohesive state, and there was no other force that could begin to do so. Thus for the first fifty years of its independence Mexico was torn asunder by strife, anarchy and confusion. Its new leaders had no commonly formulated political theory for the development of a nation-state. Some of them were unpractical idealists, some were just adventurers and some were plain bandits. But Mexico's special socio-political problems may have been impervious to solution. The agrarian situation could not be met by the application of techniques evolved by Europe's urban workers. There was no middle class. The wealthy Creoles and Spaniards were blindly interested in maintaining their own luxurious way of life and hostile to any kind of economic or social reform that would interfere with it. The Indians were kept in a state of debt and subjection to the haciendados; this, combined with an instinctive recoil to tribal divisiveness and a national treasury kept empty by wars and unrest, made the situation all but impossible.

Every intelligent person, of course, recognized the need for reform. Reform became and still is the most common word in the Mexican national and political vocabulary. But the few leaders who were able and honest enough to suggest workable programs of reform were not listened to; political opponents did not listen to or respect each other's opinions. Polarization was the order of the day, and while bloody revolutions were the accepted approach to reform, the gun became a respected instrument in the reform process. Then following the revolutions came the reform laws and constitutions. Well-motivated, high-sounding and vividly expressed testaments of the rights of one group of citizens, the constitutions invariably wiped out those of others, and one of the others was always the Church.

As early as the 1830's Gomez Farias would have crippled the Church by his kind of legislation. The Juarez, Iglesias and Lerdo laws of the mid-1800's would have not merely separated Church and State and abolished many of the Church's privileges, that would have been a good thing; but their laws would have, in one fell swoop, reduced the Church to total impotence, wiping out its charitable institutions, depriving the people of its consolations and robbing the priests and religious of their elementary rights as citizens. The reform laws written into the several constitutions, including those of 1857 and 1917, were also used to justify the most outrageous forms of cruelty, vandalism, theft and murder. Following the reforms of the 1850's, for example, bishops were banished, priests killed, churches looted; cultural, scholastic and welfare institutions were destroyed or expropriated, the spoils in many cases going into the hands of the wealthy or the pillagers themselves.

But where did the Church come into this picture? Tragically, it had been so interwoven with the state from its inception in the Latin Americas that it felt incapable of extricating itself from the conservatives, the Establishment, the wealthy, the colonial-minded. Instead of being the hopeful and transforming element in the intolerable socio-political situation, it was the expected reactionary. It didn't know how to be progressive, even in the good sense. It could not conceive of itself as operating in a different political milieu, it could not see itself carrying out its mission or its responsibilities without its huge buildings, its monasteries, hospitals and charitable institutions.

The Church, of course, has to be institutionalized; it has to have material resources to fulfill its mission but, tragically, in Mexico it was considered a vital part of the hated system. Its priests, and especially its bishops, were represented as having a vested interest in keeping the wealthy alive and the poor, poor. Add to this the fact that when Mexico became independent the vast majority of the bishops were Spanish-born and were opposed to independence, and the Church supported Maximilian, as it was to support Porfirio Diaz later on. Its clergy had been immune from court action by the civil authorities. It controlled hospitals, schools, welfare institutions. It was incapable of recognizing the most elementary form of Church-State separation. It considered the word "socialism" evil. It excommunicated those participating in the reforms and it made no attempt to reach any kind of accommodation with them.

After the fall of Juarez' successor, Lerdo, Porfirio Diaz imposed peace. Diaz was an honest, tough, insensitive man who was determined to rebuild Mexico from its bankruptcy and confusion. To do this he had to encourage foreign and domestic investors. But he allowed Indian common lands to be sold and made little or no improvement in the workers' lot. Too often they did not receive a living wage and were kept at bay by an armed constabulary when they attempted to openly rebel or protest their intolerable condition. Diaz managed to remain in office for a third of a century, and was the first president who brought stability and respect to the country. The Church backed him, not because he was giving it any special favors, but because he brought stability and he did not activate the laws which would have put it out of existence. It was during his time, January 13th, 1891, that Miguel Pro was born.

Miguel and Josefina Pro lived in Guadalupe, a delightful little suburb of Zacatecas. They were a middle-class, part-Indian family; their oldest son, Miguel, and his two sisters, Concepcion and Luz, were baptized in the chapel of the historical Franciscan monastery where their great-uncle, Father Gomez, one of Mexico's best-known missionaries, was onetime guardian. The other members of Miguel's family were Maria, Josefina, Roberto and Edmundo. A civil engineer, Miguel senior got a government appointment with the Bureau of Mines soon after young Miguel's birth, and moved immediately to the miserable, bedraggled village of Concepcion del Oro in the northeast of their home state of Zacatecas. An obvious disadvantage of Concepcion del Oro was the absence of a decent educational facility. There wasn't even a high school tutor in the community. Miguel hadn't finished high school and the two attempts to keep him in boarding school had failed because of his illness and homesickness. He was a clever lad, however, with great musical skill, a fine memory and a special competency in his father's kind of work.

There was another trait which Miguel Pro possessed and which made the squalid village life of Concepcion more tolerable than it would have been for most families. He, and his parents also, had an extraordinary interest in the miners and their families. They took care of them when they were sick, ran a little hospital for their convenience and had them visit their home. Miguel felt an especial warmth for them, and the miners responded to his perpetual smile and notorious pranks. He went down with them into the mines, he carried food and clothing to them when they were sick and he invited them to his music sessions, in which he played the guitar and in which his oldest sisters were soloists. While Miguel's interest in the poor was instinctive, a heritage of the family, he seems to have always recognized the despair, futility and dreadful social consequences that can eventuate where masses of people are condemned to poverty in the midst of plenty.

The family left the village for two extended periods while the father remained with the miners. They lived in Saltillo, a good-sized city in the neighboring state of Coahuila. It had both a high school and a grammar school which the youngsters attended, and during their second period of residence there they were neighbors of the Jesuit College of San Juan. In Saltillo the Pros had a number of close family friends, they participated in some of the town's social events, and Miguel's humor, music ability, wit, poetry and practical pranks made him very popular, not only with his contemporaries, but with all ages. It was in Saltillo that little Josefina died at thirteen years of age; the family remembered how Miguel took the father's place in those lonely days and how consciously he struggled to fill the void made by his little sister's death.

The people in the area noticed that among his constant interests were the miners and workers; he was very concerned about the social conditions in Mexico. The Pros were among the few who were conscious of the vast gap between the rich and the poor. They were sensitive also to the restiveness of the workers. They had seen examples of rioting by half-starving men who were trampled on and shot by the horsemen of the national constabulary.

Outwardly an extrovert, young Pro had a haunting concern for a lot of things which he revealed only in occasional talks with his two older sisters, or some of his closer friends. Once when visiting the mother's family in Guadalupe, Concepcion noticed how interested her brother was in the records of the old monastery. "Wouldn't it be great," he said, "to be a saint like him?" as he pointed to the handwriting of Father Gomez. But during that same visit he was determined to participate in the bull fight at the local fiesta, and had to be stopped by his sisters. Coincidentally, the young man who fought the bull was so badly gored that he had to have immediate surgery and Miguel spent hours with him during his recovery.

The two older sisters entered the convent in 1910. This seemed to have affected Miguel quite a bit. Up to now he had taken out some girls of his own age and participated in the normal social life of the community. But his sisters, who were so close to him, couldn't help noticing how intensely he questioned them on the whole idea of vocations to the religious life. When they visited their home, to be sponsors at little Humberto's First Communion, Miguel confided to them that he had given a lot of thought to his own vocation, and was contemplating entering the Jesuits. He had apparently selected one of the Fathers next door as his counsellor and the family had noticed that after his discussions with the Father, Miguel would appear quite frustrated. It may be that the Jesuits were determined that he should be sure of what he was doing and, as was the case in those days, they probably gave him very little encouragement. He was, however, accepted by the Order, received his parents' blessing and entered Hacienda El Llano, the Michoacan novitiate, on August 10th, 1911. His father was present when he received his Habit on the Feast of the Assumption that year.

Miguel's fellow novices remembered him as a good-humored but interiorly serious young man. Father Pulido, a friend of his, described him as "the one who played and prayed, the one of the pranks and the one of silence, the one who played tricks on others and helped others, the one who spent hours before the Blessed Sacrament." He appears to have been quite happy in the novitiate, although his country was entering what has been aptly called its "Via Dolorosa." Madero had succeeded in toppling Porfirio Diaz, but being a reasonably moderate man, the one possibility which terrified him was that of a revolution; he seemed to sense its demonic possibilities; but, alas, he was not the man to stop it.

If Miguel were outside the novitiate at that time he might be plunged head and shoulders in the innumerable attempts that were being made by young Catholics, both lay and clerical, to bring about some kind of radical but peaceful social reform. It was 1911, the first year that a Catholic party came to life in Mexico and was able to pose as such. All over the country social action groups were being formed by priests like Father Medina, a young Jesuit with a European background; they were familiar not only with the most up-to-date theories of social reform, but with techniques for their implementation. Those groups were especially active in the major metropolitan areas, although they were studying ways of confronting Mexico's special agrarian problems. They had plans for local co-ops, banks, the raising of money for the purchase of land and so on. But the intransigence of the haciendados, the poverty of the workers, the thirst for vengeance, revolution, immediate action on the part of those who were kept down by Diaz, the radical anticlericalism, the rejection of Christianity by the contemporary generation and its replacement by communism, facism and nationalism, all combined to smother the Church's first major effort at social reform.

Madero, the old-time liberal and moderate, was overthrown (and assassinated) by Huerta, his generalisimo, and revolution in its worst forms broke out all over the country. The Church had opposed Madero and cooperated with Huerta, feeling that he was strong enough to stabilize the country; that position proved another example of its short-sightedness and inflexibility. Carranza, Villa, Zapata and Obregon, all protesting Huerta's seizure of power and fighting under the banner of constitutionalism, turned the country into a morass of looting, pillage and murder. No city or town escaped their merciless banditry. They ransacked the churches, they assembled the priests and demanded under pain of death and/or banishment enormous ransoms from them; the bishops were thrown out, their houses wrecked and the Church records were in some cases burned or thrown all over the place. Villa, a universally recognized scoundrel, set the pace.

There were some idealists in the revolution, but, as in other revolutions and civil wars, the tenuous layer that separates all of us from pure savagery was eroded, so that hatred, vengeance and sheer blaggardism tore the country assunder. The Church paid a terrible price for Mexico's uneven social conditions; it certainly had not caused those conditions; but its apparent unawareness of them, indeed, the very fact that it numbered no kind of revolutionary in its own ranks, was proof to too many that it didn't know what was going on. What happened in Mexico may be helping today's Third World Church to realize that it is and must ever be the Church of the oppressed and poor; it must never again identify itself with the establishment, if the establishment is unjust, or as if the establishment were inviolable.

The Jesuit Fathers had resolved to continue their novitiate, but it was impossible. When Villa took over Saltillo he seized the Jesuit College, assembled the Fathers and threatened them with torture, murder and banishment if they did not come up with impossible sums of money. The Carrancistas were closing in on El Llano; on August 14th, 1914, just three years after Miguel had gone there, the rector assembled the students for its last Mass. The house was to be closed down, he told them, the students must leave immediately, they would try to keep in contact; but, as of now, everything was in God's hands. It was a lonely, rainy evening as two-by-two the young men, dressed in the attire of local Indians, wandered forever from their house of prayer. Some had arranged to stay with families; that night they hid in cornfields, strutted with affected casualness, or dropped to the ground at the sound of gunfire.

Miguel made his way to Guadalajara. His family was already dispossessed, his father had fled for his life, his mother and the younger ones were living in a one-room apartment. He was able to give some consolation to them; he could meet with some of his fellow students and they were able to have the direction of one of the padres who followed them from the novitiate. Pro and five others were ordered to go to the United States via Laredo, Texas; they wound up in the Jesuit novitiate in Los Gatos, California, and after a few months there they continued their studies in Granada, Spain.

During Miguel's four years in Granada, where he found the studies quite difficult, he was a part-time catechist for groups of youngsters in several villages in the area. But his interest in games and sports, his sense of humor, his musical talents and his ability to really share the feelings of others made him a popular and effective teacher. He kept close to the children's families, including their parents, and got the feel of their workaday lives; it was part of him.

In 1919 Miguel was sent to Nicaragua's Granada to teach in the Jesuit high school. Meanwhile, the murder and pillaging was continuing in Mexico; the 1917 constitution, the most anticlerical in Mexico's history, was being aggressively implemented. All forms of religious expression were being outlawed; religious vows were illegal, religious groups could not hold property, priests in the active ministry were losing their political rights, priests born outside the country were being banished and individual states were given the right to limit the number of priests, allowing in some cases one or two for whole cities. The bishops were fleeing the country and hundreds of Catholic schools were being closed. Carranza, now president (1917-20), realized the fanatical character of what was going on; though extremely anticlerical, he would have modified the religious persecution, but was simply unable to do so.

While Miguel must have been heartbroken with the conditions in his native Mexico, he made no reference to them in his letters to Spain. His job was to help his students grow, and that's what he wrote about. "We have to examine our dormitories for snakes and scorpions," he wrote to a Spanish friend. "I was up and down all night moving the beds from the larger leaks in the roof and comforting the youngsters who were terrified by the thunder and lightning." And a student wrote home, "When it gets too hot for baseball, or we get homesick, Padre Miguel plays the guitar and sings funny songs for us." Padre Miguel conducted classes also for the people who were doing the domestic work in the school. After two years in Nicaragua he returned to Spain, this time to the Sarria Jesuit Theologate, Barcelona, where he lived from 1922 to 1924. The Fathers noticed that despite a serious stomach ailment he had now adjusted well to study and was an above-the-average student. Because of his interest in sociology they sent him to their Enghien House in Belgium for special studies.

Belgium was quite a change. His new colleagues were French, English, German, etc. The classes were in Latin and the local language was French, of which Miguel had only a skimpy knowledge. Despite this, the men who remembered him there were impressed with his warmth and interest in what was going on; he even arranged ball games between the Americans and Europeans: "Calles against Coolidge," he called them. (Calles had now taken over in Mexico; Carranza, Villa and the others were dead.) Miguel's health was extremely bad at this point. He looked very ill, but it was decided that he should be ordained anyway. "I am saying my first Mass tomorrow," he wrote to a friend in Nicaragua, "it will be the biggest day of my life." He was sick, his country was caught in the agony of war, he was away from home and unfluent in the local language; it must have been lonely for him to spend that "biggest day" in those conditions, but he didn't complain.

After Ordination Padre Pro applied for permission to visit the Charleroi coal mines in Belgium, to meet the workers and observe the conditions there. He also joined the Catholic Worker youth movement and participated in their Social Study Week the month after his Ordination. "I want to arm myself with all the information I can," he said, "I want to learn newer techniques so I can missionize the laborers and the underprivileged in my country."

His health had reached the point where his superiors were afraid he couldn't survive. They sent him to a sanitarium where he spent six months and had three serious operations. It was while he was in the sanitarium that he learned of his mother's death. "I was never so sure of anything," he said, "than of the fact that she is now taking care of us in Heaven." He commented also on the comfort and companionship of religious community life, referring with gratitude to an old Jesuit who used to spend hours with him while he was ill. Both the sisters and doctors remarked on how he never complained of pain, but his personal physician seemed doubtful as to whether he would recover at all. It was decided, however, that he should come back to Mexico, and he arranged to spend a few days in Lourdes on the way home. He boarded the S.S. Cuba in the French port of Saint-Nazaire on June 4th, 1926 and, typically, on the way he acted as a chaplain to the crew.

When he returned to Mexico he commented on the beautiful trip and "the most strange thing of all," he said, "I didn't have even to check through customs." Despite his illness, which he mentioned only once or twice during his sixteen months in Mexico, he threw himself into a massive spate of work that was to end only in jail and death. "Father Miguel Pro's year and a quarter as a priest in his native Mexico was a godsend to countless thousands," was how his superior described it. He himself was aware of some of his advantages. He was young and vibrant despite his illness, he was capable of dressing in any disguise, he was personable, totally courageous and simply indifferent to death. When priests couldn't appear in public, he was able to keep going. His seemingly inborn and totally consecrated love for working people had extraordinary opportunities for expression in the Mexico he came home to, and he relished them.

Father Pro's country was now run by Calles, the Nero of Mexico, as he was called, and the worst Church-hater in its history. Calles' whole background seemed to dispose him for a singular hatred of the Church. Impulsive, tyrannical, completely insensitive to other people's feelings, he started as an assistant elementary school teacher, got a minor job in a city treasury from which he was fired, administered a hotel run by his brother, went into business for himself and took a small political office to help him in it. He enlisted in the revolutionary group headed by Carranza, joined forces later with the now powerful Obregon (president between 1920 and 1924), climbed up the military and political ladder rapidly until he got to the point where he could alternate power between Obregon and himself, and thus control the destinies of Mexico. Extending the 1917 constitution to its ultimate oppressiveness, he pursued priests as if they were evil things.

Father Pro was quite conscious of Calles' bigotry but he was totally unalarmed by it. He worked with truck drivers, plumbers, office workers. He took care of the poor, leasing houses where he kept a hundred hungry people at a time, supplying them with food and clothing. He said Masses in homes, heard Confessions for hours at a time. "From the first day my confessional was a riot," he told a fellow Jesuit, "I kept it warm from five to eleven in the morning and three-thirty to eight in the evening. I fainted a couple of times, but I kept going. There were all those talks and all that counselling the people needed."

The persecution under Calles was so devilish that the bishops decided to close the churches down, hoping to incite the people to rise against him. But, alas, the Mexicans were not well enough organized, nor were many of them that much concerned about the sacramental life of the Church. "With the closing of the churches," Miguel wrote, "I thought I might relax a bit. But with the increasing anxiety of the people to receive the Sacraments I couldn't." He took over a parish from Father Oton and gave retreats. No single phase of the priestly apostolate escaped him. On September 21st, 1927 at a Mass for a community of nuns, Father Pro asked, "Will you please pray that God may grant me the favor of being a victim of Calles in the cause of the faith, for the salvation of our country and for the benefit of our priests. I'm offering Mass for this intention this morning."

In October three hundred political opponents of the government, including two who submitted their names for the presidency, were openly murdered. Father Pro continued his work. He had picked up several abandoned children on his rounds, the last one he had to give to his sister. On November 13th he was in Mexico City with his two brothers, Edmundo and Roberto, and his sister. That day a bomb had been thrown at General Obregon's car. The car from which it was thrown was once owned by his brother, Roberto. It had been sold, but was still registered under Roberto's name. Obregon escaped injury, and the people who jumped from the car were eventually captured, subjected to desperate torture and killed. Although Obregon's bodyguard identified the occupants of the car from which the bombs were thrown, the Pro brothers were picked up in the black of night. The house in which they were staying was surrounded, the door broken down and the soldiers burst in with drawn revolvers. A perfectly controlled Father Miguel met them, gave absolution to everyone around, and remarked calmly, "From here on in we are giving our lives for our faith and our country. Pray that God will accept our sacrifice."

Father Pro and his brothers were taken to the police station. There was no evidence that he was in any way connected with the assassination attempt. In fact, the fourth member of the bomb group, an engineer, on hearing of the Pro brothers' arrest gave himself up, confessing that he was the one who designed and threw the bombs at Obregon's car. The chief of police, though a bigoted anticleric, was aware of the Pros' innocence and, realizing the glaring injustice of publicly executing men without trial or evidence, contacted his lawyer in the hope he could find a way out. Obregon, an anticlerical also, was happy to see his attackers tortured and annihilated, but did not want the Pros murdered in this way. Meanwhile the Argentine Ambassador and some prominent Mexicans contacted both Obregon and Calles, asking that the Pros be released. But there was a priest involved and Calles was not about to let him go. Cruz, the hardened police chief, was actually stunned when Calles, despite all the protests, ordered him to shoot Father Pro and his brother and to invite representatives of the government, as well as of the national and foreign press, to witness the shooting.

The prison yard was full of people the morning Father Miguel was led out among the photographers and reporters. He was not told where he was going. He carried his crucifix in his hand. A shadowy figure was seen approaching him: "Father," he said, "I crave your pardon for my part in this." It was the detective who helped to track him down. "No need for pardon," Father Pro said quietly, "I thank you from my heart." "Is there anything you wish?" he was asked by an army major. "Yes," Father Pro said, "just to pray." He dropped to his knees, crossing himself slowly, and extending his arms as the photographers' cameras clicked. He kissed the little crucifix and rose. Refusing to use the blindfold, he faced his killers with Christlike serenity, proclaiming with quiet, awesome dignity, "Long live Christ the King!"